The Soulwork of Justice

The Soulwork of Justice
Four Movements for Contemplative Action

WESLEY GRANBERG-MICHAELSON

Maryknoll, New York 10545

Founded in 1970, Orbis Books endeavors to publish works that enlighten the mind, nourish the spirit, and challenge the conscience. The publishing arm of the Maryknoll Fathers and Brothers, Orbis seeks to explore the global dimensions of the Christian faith and mission, to invite dialogue with diverse cultures and religious traditions, and to serve the cause of reconciliation and peace. The books published reflect the views of their authors and do not represent the official position of the Maryknoll Society. To learn more about Maryknoll and Orbis Books, please visit our website at www.orbisbooks.com.

Copyright © 2025 by Wesley Granberg-Michaelson.

Published by Orbis Books, Box 302, Maryknoll, NY 10545-0302.

Scripture quotations are from the New Revised Standard Version Bible, copyright © 1989 National Council of the Churches of Christ in the United States of America. Used by permission. All rights reserved worldwide.

All rights reserved.

No part of this publication may be reproduced or transmitted in any form or by any means, electronic or mechanical, including photocopying, recording, or any information storage or retrieval system, without prior permission in writing from the publisher.

Queries regarding rights and permissions should be addressed to: Orbis Books, P.O. Box 302, Maryknoll, NY 10545-0302.

Manufactured in the United States of America.

Manuscript editing and typesetting by Joan Weber Laflamme

Library of Congress Cataloging-in-Publication Data

Names: Granberg-Michaelson, Wesley author
Title: The soulwork of justice : four movements for contemplative action / Wesley Granberg-Michaelson.
Identifiers: LCCN 2025016054 (print) | LCCN 2025016055 (ebook) | ISBN 9781626986282 trade paperback | ISBN 9798888660836 epub
Subjects: LCSH: Granberg-Michaelson, Wesley | Reformed Church in America—Clergy—Biography | Christianity and justice
Classification: LCC BX9543.G73 A3 2025 (print) | LCC BX9543.G73 (ebook) | DDC 284/.273—dc23/eng/20250609
LC record available at https://lccn.loc.gov/2025016054
LC ebook record available at https://lccn.loc.gov/2025016055

To be a Christian is to be a contemplative, and a revolutionary.

—name unknown (Dominican preacher visiting the Potter's House, December 13, 1975, Washington DC)

Don't just do something, stand there.

—Daniel Berrigan

Contents

Foreword by Adam Russell Taylor   ix

I. An Invitation to Social Activists   1

II. Your Leap of Change   15
    A Transforming Path   19
    The Challenge of Self-Discovery   23

III. Holding the Space   27
    Working the Path   35
    Four Primal Patterns   38

IV. From Self-Sufficiency to Belonging   45
    The Refiner's Fire Burns   53
    A Crucible of Emptiness and Love   56
    Analyzing the Inner Journey   58
    Encountering Emptiness   60
    Belonging to God   63
    Belonging as the Starting Point   69

V. From Certainty to Connection   75
    Losing Belief in Beliefs   80
    Faith after Doubt   87
    Discovering Experiences of Connection   90
    Sacramental Connections   95
    Living in Sacred Spaces   98

VI. From Grandiosity to Authenticity   103
    Engaging the Enneagram   106
    Pride Evolving into Grandiosity   109
    Noticing the Signs, Listening to Dreams   113
    Grandiosity before a Fall   117
    Strength through Weakness?   119
    As the Beloved   123
    Living Authentically, Hearing a Call   126
    Hearing Wisdom from Other Voices   129
    Liberating Your True Self   132

VII. From Control to Trust   135
    Three Unexpected Disruptions   138
    The Illusion of Control   141
    How Structure Can Bring Freedom   146
    The Painful Path of Relinquishment   148
    The Deconstruction of Dreams   152
    Beckoned to Live in Trust   156
    The Final Letting Go   161

VIII. Gathered Wisdom   167
    What Difference Will Your Holding Space Make?   173
    Eight Roots to Ground Your Action for Justice   176

Epilogue: Your Anchorhold   197

Sources   205

Acknowledgments   211

Foreword

Adam Russell Taylor

In the last election cycle, like many, I went through a time when my inner life felt barren even as I felt an increasing sense of desolation and anxiety steal my joy and warp my perspective. In this spiritual and existential crisis, I recalled the advice Rev. Wes Granberg-Michaelson had given me years earlier during a time in which I was also searching for spiritual rootedness and a clearer connection to my call.

Wes encouraged me to go on retreat, when a speaking engagement at Ghost Ranch in New Mexico was unexpectedly cancelled, so I could focus on my inward journey. I reluctantly took his advice, spending four days in my first silent retreat. In the rugged beauty of the New Mexico desert, through solitude, prayer, contemplation, and communing with God's creation I was able to deepen my inward journey and wrestle with questions that led to deeper discernment and a spirit-led decision to leave a heady job leading faith engagement at the World Bank Group and rejoin Sojourners at a time in which our nation's soul and democratic system felt in peril.

In many ways the spiritual guidance that Wes offered was a precursor to insights he offers in this timely and essential book. Just as Wes's deep wisdom and spiritual guidance have been a true gift to me throughout many stages of my faith and vocational journey, Wes has now made this gift available to everyone in the pages that follow.

There couldn't be a better time for the release of this book. This perilous political season will test and stretch our nation and world in profound—and in some cases unprecedented—ways as we face a growing climate crisis, the resurgence of Christian nationalism, and the increasing threat of authoritarian governance in the United States and around the world. In these days of growing polarization, many of us struggle to find community and belonging, surrounded as we are with social media pressures, increasing acrimony, and the burgeoning use of AI. These perilous times call for the kind of courage and resilience that is so often found in and renewed by the inward journey. And increasingly that journey must be connected to the outward witness and activism that will be so desperately needed in the months and years ahead.

At Sojourners, a central charism is the interdependence of the potent synergy between spiritual renewal and social justice. As a faith-inspired activist, the commitment to spiritual renewal doesn't come naturally or easily for me. But I've increasingly become convinced that the inward journey is essential for sustaining and strengthening our outward witness. For that reason I'm so grateful for the ways that Wes, in this book, draws from the deep well of his own faith story and inward journey, sharing and gleaning wisdom from some of his most intimate and vulnerable experiences and lessons learned through a career that has spanned the highest levels of Congress to roles as a denominational leader, chair of the board at Sojourners, to life in community at Church of the Saviour.

While taking time for the inward journey can sometimes feel like a luxury we can't afford or as overly contemplative in nature, I love the way that this book is an answer to those concerns. It is highly practical, helping us to deepen our prayer life, embrace the importance of getting away, and explore who we are by uncovering our shadow, even as we intentionally engage in deeper and more intentional community.

This book will help readers better seek and find what the great theologian and mystic Howard Thurman described as the "sound of the genuine" within us, enabling all of us more faithfully to advance "God's kingdom come, on earth as it is in heaven." This book is also a generous invitation and roadmap to experience, as Wes writes, "a life rich in belonging, a life filled with sacred connection, a life nurturing your authenticity, and a life brimming with indefatigable trust."

My hope and prayer is that by engaging in a deeper inward journey, all of us can experience the type of life Wes describes, enabling and empowering us to build God's beautiful Beloved Community of justice and agape love.

I.

An Invitation to Social Activists

Dorothy Day, when talking about her life's work for social change, once described what she was up against as "a filthy, rotten system." It's an indictment easily alienating others, but in our hearts we know this to be true. You and I really don't need convincing. The repetitive litany of global realities holding our future hostage becomes mind-numbing. A climate crisis now appears irreversible, already inflicting its suffering on those least responsible for its cause. Growing global income inequality dwarfs the gains made in combating grinding poverty. Endless resource extraction pretends limits are nonexistent and portends conflicts over scarce raw materials. An economic system is riveted to reward short-term greed over long-term sustainability. Rising nationalistic autocracies are fueled by religious sanctification of racial superiority.

And more.

Violence and wars are spawned by the grandiosity of unaccountable rulers motivated by greed, pride, and imperial myths. Journalists are imprisoned and killed for revealing truth. Bigotry and racism are embraced as effective political strategies. Guns outnumber people in countries calling themselves civilized. Health and well-being are determined by the money in one's pocket rather than the needs of one's body.

Prisons are run for profit in a novel form of social enslavement for millions, mostly people of color. Indigenous people struggle for identity against the legacy of cultural and physical genocide. Pervasive social media fuels profits by feeding addictive attraction to violence, exploitative sex, and hate. Refugees swarm the globe, becoming pawns of politicians rather than persons with dignity.

And then there's the church.

The incarnate life of Jesus seems long forgotten, with his Father's name used to justify nationalistic glory, imperialistic conquest, military campaigns, white supremacy, and prideful arrogance. We can "stand our ground" with "God on our side." And the victims cry out, those who feel orphaned, forgotten, and forsaken by the church. The survivors of abuse, whose witness was repressed and mocked. The hidden graves behind schools intended to impose white Christian civilization on "natives." Cries and laments echo among desperate migrants gathering to pray and break bread, and among prison inmates reading their bibles and yearning for justice. Against the backdrop of global injustice and climate catastrophe, we can point, with former President George H. Bush, to "a thousand points of light." Many of you have helped them shine. But honestly, those lights seem dim against a million points of repression. Yes, forever in the life of God's people we can look to a faithful few, to committed communities and movements, to sacred and secular saints, who have maintained a prophetic allegiance to what they have heard from God and seen in Jesus. They have persevered amid societies that have become numb to transcendent values and a church that seems deaf to the words it pronounces each week. It seems so hard for the words of Jesus to be heard by most of those who claim his name. But some, a minority, have tried hard to listen.

I know all these things to be true, as I suspect you do. Yet you and I are propelled to seek change, to pursue social, political, economic, cultural, and religious transformation. At some level we can't get that out of our system. It's been implanted within us, hopefully by the Holy Spirit. "Your kingdom—or your *kin-dom*—come, your will be done, on earth as it is in heaven." We don't just pray this—if we still pray this prayer at all. We believe our lives must be lived for that purpose. Most likely we're comfortable being called activists. Or if, like me, you haven't spent most of your life marching in the streets but rather working within institutions, organizations, and churches, you're there because you've pursued opportunities for change and transformation.

Maybe you share this implanted passion for transformational change in our society and world, believing this must happen. But this change must also include change in ourselves. It must include ongoing attention to your inward journey. You'll need to recognize not only the overwhelming weight of oppression from without, but also the perils and destructive threats that emerge from within. Your inner life will require an ongoing exploration as rigorous as your excavation of the external, global structures of oppression and social sin. In the end, if your inward and outward journey become interwoven, your life and witness will have opportunity to flourish. But if they are alienated from each other, and your inward journey is neglected or rejected, your outward journey, regardless of the intensity of your commitment, eventually will start to disintegrate, with self-inflicted wounds that are likely to badly injure others and undermine the causes to which you have committed your lives.

I don't expect you to take my word for it. You probably already know that depleting one aspect of your life and personhood affects all others. But if like me, you live in the hope that perhaps something might connect you with your life's experience, then I'd be filled with gratitude if sharing the wandering course of my own journey might suggest pathways for you that help avoid the dead ends I've encountered, or at least assist you in navigating similar perils.

> *My hope is that each of you . . . will be sustained and emboldened in your participation in the world's transformation.*

Each of our journeys is filled with grace and pain. But only the pain we name can be transformed. The pain we don't name—refuse to name—will be transmitted. My hope is that each of you will become secure enough, and brave enough, to face the pain that will become the occasion for your own transformation. And that from this ongoing insurrection of grace, you will be sustained and emboldened in your participation in the world's transformation.

In 2017, on a year-end retreat, the leader asked what descriptive name we might like to claim for the coming year.

I thought a bit and said "elder," the way Indigenous elders in communities across the globe share wisdom. When I was asked why, I smiled: "Because I could share wisdom without taking responsibility." It was humorous, but serious too.

In my life I've had my share of taking responsibility for things in ways that have been rare privileges. I was the legislative director for a US senator working against the Vietnam war. In Montana I started an institute committed to strengthen the churches' care for the earth. At the World Council of Churches I directed its work on church and society, including beginning its work on climate change. Then my denomination, the Reformed Church in America, selected me to be its chief executive as general secretary. I played an important role in beginning and directing Christian Churches Together, served as chair of the board of Sojourners and as president of the Global Christian Forum Foundation, so I had plenty of chances to take responsibility for organizations and movements. And all have involved grace and pain.

But those chapters, at this point in my journey, have ended, even as I hold with you this calling of social change and transformation. I have some insights to share, where maybe you are on another place in the long journey of soulwork and justice. Maybe early days, new roads, big challenges that are so daunting. And I want to share that with you because it's with you that my hope lies, that our shared faith in God holds forward into what God is guiding. Penultimately, in a very real way, that hope is focused on your future journeys. God's Spirit has implanted this passion for the change that

God desires and intends for God's world within your hearts. I pray that it may flourish.

Most of us begin the journey of that hope for transformation with questions. How do I go forward? What should I do? And what do I need? Some things I've learned that I'd like to share, things about developing an integrated life, but also some of the best avenues and practices I know to do so.

Honestly, this won't be easy. You'll be going up against evil every day. Monstrous evil, overwhelmingly present for all to see. And subtle evil, embedded within the efficient and self-justifying institutions claiming our temporal allegiance. All that takes a toll, because we're fighting not just against flesh and blood, but against principalities, powers, and rulers of darkness. Our movements for social transformation require political actions and economic strategies. But at the heart of it all they require a spiritual engagement. That can only be met by an inward journey that is integrated with our outward mission.

You'll need some tools. Here's the thing. Your inner life will go dormant, and become unconsciously dangerous, if it's ignored or neglected. It requires your intentional attention. Years ago, a wise retreat leader told me, "Prayer is attention." Today, incessant pressures automatically consume our consciousness through the continuous onslaught of information delivered by devices that seem hinged to our minds. Our attention gets riveted on the latest "breaking news" and the juiciest one-liners from celebrities. We live in an "attention economy" in which algorithms push our eyes toward externally intense events for profit. It requires discipline to redirect this attention to the inner life of your soul.

So, *learn to pray*. I don't mean prayer that adds to the billions of tasks God is being requested to do. Rather, prayer that gradually places the core of your being in the presence of God's love. That's how you can feel safe and secure. And that's essential for being strong and brave in the active work for change you're called to do. This doesn't come naturally. You'll need to learn through trying, through doing. The tools, the language, and the techniques are all available. Centering prayer. Contemplative prayer. Lectio Divina. Silence. Meditation. Walking prayers. The Jesus Prayer. All these pathways are there to help center your soul, to open your heart, to ground your identity.

Then, *get away*. Physically go off to a place where you can emotionally detach from all that weighs you down, and all that is left undone. Retreat centers, usually at monasteries, became the homes for my heart, whether in the Shenandoah mountains of Virginia, by the lakes of Michigan, in the hills of New Jersey, amid the Rockies of Colorado, on the desert of New Mexico, or by Lake Neuchâtel in Switzerland. Find the place where your heart can feel at home. Retreat to there. You'll be helped to divest yourself from what immediately overwhelms you. You'll probably discover how to become engaged more deeply in facing the menacing evil that confronts you, within and without. And you'll be replenished with restored clarity and recovered grace.

Explore who you are. Figure out how you are inwardly wired. Uncover your shadow, your dark side. Discover your unique giftedness, the essence of what your presence can bring. You will need help to do so, but again, all the tools are there. Learn about your Enneagram type. Take the Myers-Briggs personality test. Do the Gallup Strength Finder. Welcome all those tests and personality inventories that can give you discerning clues about who God uniquely created you to be. Please don't become one of those activists and leaders who think they can do it all, and whose blindness to their own flaws projects judgments and pain onto others. If you're stuck, get into therapy. Drop the illusion that your inner life doesn't need any repair.

Journal. Take pen to paper and try. For five decades that's how I've processed the pain and grace in my life. It might work for you. *Markings,* the journal of Dag Hammarskjöld, the general secretary of the United Nations, was published after his death. He characterized it as "a sort of white book describing my negotiations with myself—and with God." We all need a means to reflect in that way and get some detachment from the ongoing turbulence of our inward journey stirring beneath our outward activism. An interrogating dialogue with our hidden self is essential for growth. And welcoming our interrogation by a gracious God is foundational for life. A journal can hold the memory and redemptive power of those conversations.

Don't go it alone. I love to go fly fishing for trout. But when I go on new, unfamiliar water, I'll hire a guide who has been on those waters and can warn me of dangers as well as preparing me for what to expect. The guide accompanies me with encouragement, insight, and correction. I find it's the same with the inward and outward spiritual journey. So, take someone with you as a guide. Someone with wisdom who can listen deeply, watch carefully, and give disarming advice skillfully. Classic traditions call this a spiritual director, and they are now proliferating, even in Protestant circles. Find one. Maybe you'll change the name to coach, or spiritual friend, or whatever. But exercise the humility to have your journey accompanied by one who can be a guide, because beyond any doubt, you will encounter troubled waters.

Worship. I'm assuming you are at least a friend of Jesus Christ and desire to be a follower. If not, you are still more than welcome as one reading these words. But this is a friendship that is always held in a community and celebrated there. That's because there are no Robinson Crusoe Christians. Together is not only better; it's definitional. Members of this gathered community remember who they are. They hear the ageless story and make it their story. In liturgy, song, word, and sharing around a common table, this happens. You should be there, to be reminded of what your story is, and to be connected in both past and present with those who share it.

Those are the tools and practices at your disposal. But they don't just happen and deploy themselves. They are not on automatic pilot. Far from it. In our society, and in many of the institutions and movements where we exercise our activism, little or none of this is intrinsic to the organizational culture.

Instead, the pressure to perform, to achieve, and to decisively make a difference mitigates against any intentional attention to our inner lives. In those places the journey is one way, only outward, and always urgent.

You will need to intervene in the decisions about what is necessary, urgent, and essential for your journey. Long ago I learned that even the best meaning, highly principled Christian organizations and movements are not going to nurture or hold you accountable for the practice and care of your inward journey. And if you burn yourself out, or lose your integrity, or suffer an emotional breakdown, or have a crisis of faith, you alone will be held responsible and bear the blame and shame. As a mentor once told me, half in jest, "No one thanks you when you have a nervous breakdown."

So, you have choices to make. You will have to choose whether your inward journey will become lodged and nurtured in your life as something as essential and regular as brushing your teeth. That means choosing the discovery of your "true self." And that is intertwined with the choice to discover where God is in your present journey, and in your life's promised and desired future. None of this will happen fast. All of this will require that you create a "holding space" where that journey with yourself and God will have the freedom to emerge and flow forward.

The tools and practices available require disciplined commitment to create this holding space for your inward and outward journey to become integrated as a whole. Prayer, retreat, self-exploration, journaling, accompaniment, and worship—these should be embodied in your practice of life. You can think of it, in fact, as a "rule of life." This means a structure of specific times, regularly observed. When do you pray? (And please don't answer in some pious, meaningless way like "all the time.") How often will you go on retreat, and where? How will you explore the inner psychological caverns of your life? When will you journal? Who will be your spiritual guide? Where and how will you worship?

You won't be able to hold yourself accountable to all this. You'll need others. Share the disciplines of your intended commitments. Don't keep them to yourself. Have a friend, or a group, or even a governing board help you keep your desired commitments. I once asked a governing board, responsible for my hiring, to make my intention to take a retreat day every month part of my performance appraisal. And I rarely missed a month because of that.

Don't hesitate. Just take a first step. The next steps will be revealed, one step at a time. But decide to walk forward.

When I was first faced with adopting regular and rigorous spiritual disciplines as part of the requirement for joining a mission group at Church of the Saviour in Washington, DC, I rebelled. It sounded legalistic, robbing me of my freedom in Christ. And my time was already so pressured, with an unjust war to stop, after all. A wise elder said to think of this like being called to be a concert pianist. You'd have to practice to fulfill your calling. Or like playing professional baseball. Consider the disciplines you'd be willing to adopt.

If your calling is to participate in God's transforming work in the world, confronting the perils of embedded evil and pernicious, grinding injustice, how can you possibly attend to those tasks without the disciplined preparation of your heart and soul? Wouldn't you be open to embracing practices that could build the holding space necessary for the deep work of transformation to be sustained in both your inward and outward journey? That's a truth I learned and practiced gradually, over many years, with false starts and periodic inattention. Yet there was enough unexpected grace to nudge me forward. My hope is that you will learn faster, and more thoroughly. The truth is that God needs you. Urgently. With a soul that is prepared and resilient.

If any parts of this message connect within you, then don't hesitate. Just take a first step. The next steps will be revealed, one step at a time. But decide to walk forward. It's a path of grace and pain, but God's grace prevails. And that grace beckons you to participate in the outpoured love of God that is flowing for the sake of the world's transformation. Joy awaits you there. And my solidarity here.

II.

Your Leap of Change

You will experience pain on your journey. How will you respond? That's the question for you to face. Processing the pain in your life and discovering what you learn from it is a lifelong quest. This will force you to abandon the illusions of what you thought you needed to make your life work. But it can open a transformational journey that can uncover your true self, rooted in the mystery of God's love.

All of us spend much of our lives constructing the protection we think we need to survive and thrive. These layers of defense work well until crisis hits and they start to crumble. At this point you face a choice: double down on the defenses, or open yourselves to the pain and discover the life that is waiting to be revealed to you. In a book by Kelley Nikondeha I first read this truth, "Only the pain we name is available for transformation."

At those moments you are faced with a leap of faith from protection to surrender—a choice life puts in front of you time and again. It can feel like the difference between life and death. You fear the pain can destroy you. But at that hour of decision, you can find the courage, or cling to the hope, that embracing what has cracked your life open can lead to your healing and to the discovery of who you are called to be.

Here's a true story from the Buddhist tradition that might illustrate this. In Bangkok, Thailand, there was huge clay statue of the Buddha. In the 1950s a combination of heat and drought caused it to begin to crack. Monks came to examine the damage. They looked at the largest crack, and then shone a flashlight on it. To their surprise, through the crack they spotted a reflection of gold. It turned out that a solid gold Buddha was embedded beneath the clay. Six-hundred years earlier layers of protective clay and plaster were used to cover up the gold Buddha and protect it from invading armies. The monks were killed, but the Buddha survived. Yet over time its identity was defined by its layers of protective covering, while its true nature was hidden from all.

Most of us are familiar with the Leonard Cohen lyric: "There's a crack in everything. That's how the light gets in." Facing the cracks, embracing the pain, and allowing the light to shine in, revealing your essence require that you develop what I call your holding space. This is your spiritual infrastructure, constructed using the tools, practices, and disciplines you've learned to embrace. That's how you will navigate the troubled waters that may seem to engulf you. Your cleverness, or intelligence, or social connections, or determination, in the end, won't suffice if you haven't curated a holding space that slowly but persistently allows pain and grace to reveal their truth, liberating your emergent life.

During the lock-down silences of the beginning of the COVID pandemic I embarked on a project suggested by my wife, Kaarin, of reading back through the personal journals I'd kept for much of my adult life—thousands of words scribbled on hundreds of pages in scores of journals for over fifty years. Through those years that's how I processed what was happening in my holding space. I discovered a repeating pattern over decades of how God used pain and disruption to break up the protective facades I clung to, slowing nudging me away from a self-centered life toward a God-centered life. You'll discover that same pattern in your own journey. It beckons you to a leap of faith. Sometimes the only assurance you have is that God is in the pain you are naming. No shortcut around the struggles is available. But grasping enough grace to enter into them is what leads to change. Step by step, you can embrace your true identity, secured in a love you can never control but always can courageously trust.

A Transforming Path

Early in our marriage, when Kaarin and I were part of Church of the Saviour in Washington, DC, she experienced a paralyzing depression. A wise older companion came to accompany her and to offer counsel, born out of a similar trauma. "I know something of what you're suffering and how devastating it feels," she said. "But perhaps you can see this as dross being consumed in a refining fire. Your true self, held in God's love, is there, wanting to emerge." Over time, through grace and pain, that is exactly what I witnessed emerging in her life. A crack let in light, discovering gold, and in this time she—and we as we journeyed together—discovered gold.

This metaphor of uncovering the gold of one's true identity is found in the Christian tradition as well. God is like "a refiner's fire," a text from Malachi (3:2) reads.

In ancient times gold embedded in rocks and dirt was crushed, washed, and then subjected to high temperatures in furnaces, removing impurities—the dross—and revealing its essence. When a metal is being purified, the goldsmith can know that its essence has been revealed when the image of his face is reflected back in the emerging material.

Destroying false protective coverings allows the emergence of what is true. Layers of dross hide your connection to being held in God's love, reflecting back the image of God. You are kept isolated from this, just as the plaster and clay shrouded the gold Buddha. This creates the illusion of a separated self, living in deluded isolation. Thomas Merton called this the "false self." Richard Rohr rephrases this as the "separate self," capturing better perhaps the subtle nuance of this mistaken identity.

My journals over many years documented how my life would pivot around values, goals, and aspirations that in our culture, and even in the subculture of our churches, appeared to me as attractive and justifiable. I doubt it's any different for you. Your self-sufficiency, your agency, your mastery, your success, your strength, your wealth, your reputation, your power—this all is the dross, the external layers that come to define your identity. Celebrity trumps character. But all this and more prospers by protecting your separation from your truest identity found through an abandonment to God's love.

The refiner's fire liberates the image of God in you. An inward spiritual process that painstakingly removes layers of dross to liberate your true essence involves pain, time, and grace. Of course, that takes a journey. If you're among those who have been to seminary, you might rehearse theological questions that pop up, maybe from old tapes. Here's my brief take. I don't believe that the trailhead for your journey, or mine, starts with being hopelessly mired in an original imprisonment of depravity that was not of our own doing. The conviction that we begin as being worthless and are always prone to prove our unworthiness, even after knowing God's grace, breeds a spirituality dominated by the constant fear of failure.

There are other grounded ways of approaching this journey. The Orthodox theological tradition, for instance, with ancient roots in the earliest centuries of Christianity's development, offers painstaking pathways in the spiritual journey to free the image of God, implanted within us, to blossom and flourish. We become true daughters and sons of God and are "participants in the divine nature" (2 Pt 1:4). Our new self is "created according to the likeness of God" (Eph 4:24). That makes us fully human. The Orthodox call this process of spiritual growth *theosis*, also expressed as deification. St. Athanasios the Great, in fourth century Egypt, stunningly put it this way: "God became man so that man might become divine." Sin and imperfection are seriously wounding; yes, there is a lot of dross. But not in ways so corrupting that God's image is virtually irretrievable. Rather, this image of divine love, resting at the core of your being, yearns to be uncovered and embodied in your flesh, like refined gold.

Your true self dwells in an intimate and expansive connection to God's love. Through that sacred portal you can be present in solidarity to all that God loves, and to the pain, brokenness, and suffering of all that seeks to resist the redemptive power of that love in the world. This is what it means to be "in Christ." The intersection of the divine and human, of the spiritual and material, fully revealed in the incarnation, is the place where your identity is discovered, where your life is beckoned, and where your belonging is secure. Your true self dwells in connection to this Life.

However, it's no small task to discover this sacred connection amid the hectic normalcy of your everyday life. The cracks in your facade are easily repressed when you're convinced that you are doing good work, even critical work. Like saving the planet, confronting racism, and stopping war. Unswerving, indefatigable commitment to a cause, with prophetic urgency, is the catalyst for social change. But if you allow such a cause to smother attention to inner motives, vulnerabilities, and ego needs, you will pay a personal price. In the end, the cause itself can be tarnished. As Richard Rohr says, "It's possible to do the right things for the wrong reasons!"

The Challenge of Self-Discovery

As I wrestled with this tension, I was drawn to a modern example of one who lived a life of action rooted in this interior connection, Dag Hammarskjöld. An extraordinary secretary general of the United Nations, Hammarskjöld's life was cut short in 1961 in an unexplained airplane crash while he was on a peacekeeping mission in Africa. After his death his journal was discovered and published as *Markings*. It reveals how Hammarskjöld was inspired by medieval mystics like Meister Eckhart and others who illuminated the Christian faith inherited from his culture and childhood. In language of his own experience, the Swedish diplomat reflected the movement from the separate self to the true self:

> *The cracks in your facade are easily repressed when you're convinced that you are doing good work, even critical work. Like saving the planet, confronting racism, and stopping war.*

> Clad in this "self," the creation of irresponsible and ignorant persons, meaningless honors and catalogued acts—strapped into the strait jacket of the immediate.
>
> To step out of all of this, and stand naked on the precipice of dawn—acceptable, invulnerable, free: in the Light, with the Light, of the Light. Whole, real in the Whole.

> Out of myself as a stumbling block, into myself as fulfillment.

He understood this journey went through a refiner's fire: "the fire of the body burns away its dross and, rising in a flame of self-surrender, consumes its closed microcosm."

If you've already become curious about the contemplative life, you've probably read the writings of authors like Thomas Merton, Howard Thurman, Thomas Keating, and Barbara Holmes, as well as classic voices like Julian of Norwich, St. John of the Cross, Teresa of Avila, and many others. Many of them lived in cloistered monastic communities and convents. Today, any desire you have to nurture an inward journey comes within the accelerated pace of your vocational life, maybe in a marriage stressed by longing for togetherness, perhaps in a family clinging to its bonds in a culture that fractures familial loyalty, and with a mind that you find is endlessly distracted by the electronic avalanche of information.

That's why the model of Dag Hammarskjöld can speak with resonance today, six decades after his untimely death. His inner journey was never an end in itself, nor was it protected by an environment extracted from the normal milieu of modern life. Rather, it undergirded and empowered a life deeply engaged in the call to heal the world's devastating wounds.

I've emphasized that the integration of contemplation and action requires practices that open one's life to those revealing, redemptive cracks that can let light in. Those practices will vary. For some this integration begins in therapy. James Finley, whose spiritual director at one time was Thomas Merton, asks this: "What happens in psychotherapy? We ask the question—how can I be vulnerable and safe while the illusions of my life are exposed?" You may need a safe space sitting opposite a therapist to explore why you cling so tenaciously to your false self.

Practices shaped by long wisdom tracing the journey of the soul can certainly help. For instance, the *examen* from the Ignatian tradition of spirituality can bring you discernment. This is a practice of prayerfully reviewing a day's experience. It includes asking: "Where do you find consolation in what you are feeling and experiencing? And where do you experience desolation?" Sometimes such simple tools can center the stream of meandering feelings and fears that arise as your true self tries to emerge.

The safe inner space your soul silently yearns for can be nurtured through long-practiced ways of spiritual formation already mentioned, such as retreats, silence, contemplative prayer, and journal writing as well as through liturgical habits, dwelling in the word, meditative readings, and music, which is the language of the soul. Other intentional practices can help liberate you from the perpetual distractions to your interior attention. You may find inward centering in a long walk to no particular destination, staring at waves cascading onto a beach, the natural float of your dry fly alluring trout close to a riverbank, the caressing warmth of water in a hot spring, or gazing at birds building a nest from a park bench in an urban center.

The practices themselves will not solve your challenges, but they can open the space in your life to sustain your inward and outward pilgrim pathway.

The refiner's fire burns in the crucible that exposes your false self to the fire of love. But when the heat gets turned up by crisis, fear and self-doubt can send you fleeing back to the illusions of safety in what you think you know. Self-exposure is frightening before it is redemptive. It is tempting to cling to the deluded self when the invitation to the authentic self requires letting go of what you thought you needed to survive.

That's why I reiterate that it's imperative for you to create the inward spiritual infrastructure to process, together, both the pain of life's struggles and the grace of healing that can flow from them. It is the room needed for your separated self to recognize the dross of your own defenses and take the leap of surrender into the purifying discovery of your true identity.

III.

Holding the Space

Unexpectedly, life can throw you into situations that test the roots of your identity, and you lack the inward center to respond. Early on in my vocational pathway, here's how it happened to me. The senator I was working for, Mark Hatfield, put the article on my desk with a note, "Congrats, Whiz!" I opened up page three of the *Washington Post,* and an article by George Wilson, its top reporter on military issues, led off the piece with my name:

> Wes Michaelson—one of the cadre of "Whiz Kids" helping their Senators make a stand against the Pentagon this year—found himself spending the night in the basement of the New Senate Office Building just before the 4th of July weekend, sorting and stapling together the pulpy pages of a booklet called "Report on Military Spending."

Along with other staff I was part of a bipartisan effort of a group of senators critiquing and opposing proposals for several new weapons systems in the Pentagon's budget. The opposition focused on reducing military spending and adjusting the nation's priorities.

Reading the article, I got an adrenaline rush. Barely a year earlier I abruptly had left Princeton seminary and at twenty-four was now a staffer trying to find my way in the corridors of political power. On that day I knew nearly every important politico in Washington was reading about me.

Alienated from an evangelical subculture that largely countenanced the raging Vietnam War, my quest for a church community had led me through the doors of Church of the Saviour, an innovative, ecumenical, mission-driven church I read about in Elizabeth O'Connor's book *Call to Commitment*. Fresh language about the "inward and outward journey," and serious spiritual practices—including retreats, silence, and journaling, all undergirding courageous outreach for justice and service to pressing social needs—immediately captured my heart's attention.

I started to learn how writing in a journal could deepen one's interior and exterior journey and took pen to paper. Only a month into this reflective process, George Wilson told me that the article was due to appear. "*I can hardly wait to see it,*" I wrote in my journal on July 31, 1969, *"but really what does it mean? . . . Most of all, what about my pride?"* What was then a glimmer of tension would for years come to consume me.

The world of social activism nurtures grandiosity. If you are part of that culture, even in smaller, local settings away from Washington, DC, you've probably witnessed this. Inward, private truths get shaded by public personalities. Wounds are repressed. Leaders are prone to creating an artificial self that is curated and promoted on social media.

We've all seen this in politics, activism, and in the church as well. Perhaps you've been a self-curator who enjoys that swell of pride. But stress tests of life can bring threatening crises, and the curated self isn't able to meet them. You can be left spiritually stranded without the inner space needed to face pain and uncover needed truth about who you actually are and who you are called to be. That described my twenty-four-year-old self when I first began putting yearnings into words on the pages of my new journal responding to reading several portions of scripture:

> July 13, 1969
> *"Springs of living water"—this is my deep, heartfelt desire—to nurture my inner spiritual life, to receive the waters of the spirit—flowing forth so that I will never thirst again. "Out of the depths." That is the issue—what is at the depths of my being? I fear there is little. Distracted by the demands of work each day, my life revolves around only the responsibilities of such external activity. There is no chance to truly develop the inner, lasting qualities of love, concern, long-suffering, etc. That is the real point. These qualities must be developed from within; at present they have no opportunity to grow.*

I was trying to develop the room for my inward journey to find its footing in the midst of life's messiness. You may glimpse the hint of a hunger and emptiness gnawing at your soul, but this is so easily covered by your insatiable habits, your addiction to cascading electronic information, and the perceived urgency of your next external action. Working for a leading antiwar senator while the Vietnam war raged, I felt trapped in the incessant grasp of such urgency.

The causes today engaging you and many others—causes as profound as resisting autocracy and saving sustainable human life on our planet—understandably feel urgent. The most difficult step is often the first one: confessing your soul's need for discovering a space to begin integrating your inward and outward journeys, knowing that to be the only sustainable foundation for our actions in the world.

Creating a safe space to hold my thirst for living water took arduous and experimental steps. Church of the Saviour had nurtured a culture of faith formation including silence, retreats, journaling, spiritual direction, accountable mission groups, and more, long before these began to infiltrate mainstream Protestantism. Early in my time there, I hesitantly signed up for a silent retreat, racing there late on a Friday that to that point had been filled with incessant action in my work at the US Senate.

The silence terrified me. We were seated around a dining table at the Dayspring Retreat Farm that evening to begin our silent retreat. Food was passed with glances, nods, and gestures. As darkness descended, I made my way on a forested path to my room, with a bed, small desk and chair, and a sink. Anxiety welled up. How could I last through a weekend without words?

Sometimes memorable words reveal truth. But often superficial words keep truths submerged. Silence can be a tool that closes the faucet of incessant ramblings, creating space for other voices to be heard, including the voice of God. That first retreat into silence began showing me tools that could create a holding space to center my soul.

It took time—a lot more time than that first retreat—for silence to become a friend. Eventually that friendship blossomed.

You may feel, as I did, resistance to embarking on such a pathway. If you come from evangelical and pietistic traditions, one reason may stem from that divide between belief and pietism and social action that has plagued the history of American Christianity. This has bred many activists who are suspicious of pietistic attention to the inner spiritual life. You may harbor those suspicions, fearing that this inward journey will divert energy away from work for justice and repress the mandate for the radical social change needed in society, and announced by Jesus, in favor of individualistic changes in your heart. But are you then simply living in reaction to a shallow pietism that blinded you to the world's wounds, and neglecting your inner life? That was my story.

In those times when denominational bureaucracy absorbed my life, I began making annual retreats before each of our general synods to St. Benedict's Monastery by Snowmass, Colorado. An architecturally inspired hermitage provided a cloistered space overlooking mountainous grandeur. The monastery was home to the late Father Thomas Keating, a modern contemplative pioneer, who retrieved and developed the practice of centering prayer. Keating also related centering prayer to the Twelve Step program of recovery. This was a way for creating a holding space while encountering the pain of life's illusions. In his book *Divine Therapy and Addiction: Centering Prayer and the Twelve Steps,* Keating explains:

> As we become aware of the shadow side of our personality and how much energy we put into programs for security, power and affection, esteem and approval, we realize that we cannot manage our own lives.

Receiving such insights, however, depends on your readiness. It's hard to predict and know what prompts you to rotate the attention of your heart toward the roots of pride, the futility of selfish striving, and the present legacy of past wounds. Often those insights come as the result of a personal and even traumatic crisis. It may begin by the irrepressible advance of quiet boredom and gnawing discontent. Or you simply yield to yearnings and soulful hungers that find no satisfaction in normalcy of your life. Musician Kae Tempest, in her latest album *The Line Is a Curve,* expresses with simple clarity what is happening in such moments: "Chin deep in a bag of white lies saying I'm sick and tired of my own advice."

A holding space allows you to break through the echo chambers of your own advice. But it's tricky, because even subconsciously you can import spiritual platitudes and pietistic formulas to sprinkle mental holy water on shallow, ego-driven aspirations. Thus, you believe your material success is a sign of God's blessing. You have an apostolic calling, and God wants to expand the zone of your influence. And you believe personal trials are brought to test your fidelity to God's work. Those opposing your work, even in the Christian community, are unwittingly being manipulated by crafty powers of darkness. The righteousness of your cause means you can expect to be a victim of persecution. Your authority, because of your gifts, discernment and calling, requires trust and holy submission from others for God's work to prosper.

There might be some strands of truth in such convictions. But the thrust of all those explanations, and many more, is that they deflect attention from your inner self—from your motives, grievances, vulnerabilities, aspirations, and wounds. All that gets projected outward on others in movements of unrecognized self-justification. You create the enemies that your inner wounds need to hide your pain. Remember, only the pain you name is available for transformation. And the pain you don't name will get transmitted onto others.

Working the Path

Learning to live with a holding space, discovering the mysteries of God's intersection with your life, will require persistent patience, disciplined practices, and undaunted courage. That is essential, at least in my experience, to sustain a resilient outward journey that can participate in the unfolding of God's preferred and promised future for the world, pursuing justice. You will need fresh language, metaphors, tools, and practices to nurture a spirituality that can navigate the inward movements of your heart to connect you to the outward work of God's Spirit, creating all things new.

In the wayward wanderings of my own journey, I struggled to create interior space amid an exterior life absorbed in causes of peacemaking, justice, environmental preservation, church renewal, ecumenism, and more. In early years it felt like I was swimming against the stream of external moral and political urgency, looming social catastrophe, and expanding self-importance. Flashes of revealing insight into the banality of my own advice, and small epiphanies of a Love holding my life's fragile center, required time to curate within a holding space.

Five years after the article featuring me in the *Washington Post* produced an infusion of grandiosity accompanied by a hint of quiet anxiety, parts of my plaster and clay facade were starting to fracture:

MAY 7, 1974, AGE 28
A lot of my unconscious pride, pretention, and self-righteousness—or more basically, the belief in my own invincibility—is all being destroyed.

People have made me into being so much that I have come to believe it. It's strange how the biblical truths about strength coming from weakness and God being close to those who are contrite and brokenhearted—how these never had much experiential meaning or significance for me. . . .

Now there is the deep sense of the utter futility of all that I do which is centered around the self and which is prompted by its demands. . . . It is encountering my own emptiness.

I lasted a dozen years in the nation's capital until the unquenched hunger of my soul and confusion over my calling beckoned me away. In Missoula, Montana, I found a church community and an environment to help center my identity more around being than doing. In time, emerging connections to my true self recentered my outward journey, leading me to the World Council of Churches in Geneva, then to leadership in my denominational home, and to frontiers of ecumenical work around the world. Throughout practices of silence remained. And journaling continued to be the chronicle for my thirst and my sporadic encounter with the mystery of God's all-embracing love.

You create the enemies that your inner wounds need to hide your pain.

Everyone's life experience and spiritual pathways are unique. Those whose pathways begin in the context of social oppression with marginalized identities may encounter different movements to liberate the image of God at their center. Yet, your specific story, plumbed to the depths, can reveal truths and illumine pathways that bring you into shared common purpose with others more than you may have previously imagined. Then the particular nature of your experience becomes a participation in the universal.

My pattern has been to find times of retreat—a day, a weekend, or whenever I could set time apart. Sometimes it was fly fishing, its own kind of silence and renewal. And my practice continued to be reading what I had written over past weeks or months, reacquainting my heart to its recent inward pathways. Then seeking to be attentive to what is, and where God is.

Your pattern may be different. Retreats at monasteries may not be your preference, or even a realistic option. But any of us can discover how and where to step into an interior silence, like Jesus, in a garden, up a mountain, on a park bench, or in a chair with a candle. You can create the space for this essential soulful work in any place that detaches you from the distractions of normalcy.

Four Primal Patterns

With tools and practices like these, what might you expect to encounter as your journey progresses? What behaviors and traits should you be attentive to which might be buried beneath your outward activism? What might you expect to encounter in the journey from the ego self and the protected self to the surrendered self?

In observing my experience and in conversation with others, I've noticed four qualities of character that can do you in, if left unattended. Namely, self-sufficiency, certainty, grandiosity, and control. If these roam and careen freely through your life, they eventually wreak havoc in your heart, wound others (including those you love), and dismantle the good you've set out to do. I've experienced that havoc, and I've seen it happen, too many times, amid causes and in the lives of colleagues whom I hold dear, whose causes and mission are just.

These four qualities are not intrinsically evil. Few things are. They are essential starter tools for developing a self strong enough to make your way in the world against all would-be defeats. They also have an attractiveness that is hard to resist—and if deceptively alluring—because they feed your "ego inflation." Self-sufficiency corrects dependence. Certainty overcomes doubt. Grandiosity corrects low self-esteem. And control combats chaos. But when these traits are put on steroids, they become unconscious compulsions.

If you allow them, they will alienate you from your truest identify. Instead, they become layers of dross, a facade of plaster and clay, the building blocks of the protected self. The more we rely on them, the more encrusted they become over our inner self, hiding ourselves from ourselves.

Here's why it's so important for you and me to grasp this. The way we are wired, enabling us to be committed activists, persuasive advocates, and effective faith leaders, means that we rely on traits like self-sufficiency, certainty, grandiosity, and control. And we will probably have a dollop of narcissism thrown into the recipe of our modus operandi. But if we ignore their seductive power, these behaviors come to control us. They get rooted deep within and become nearly impregnable.

Here's what happens. Our self-sufficiency, which works well because we are smart and talented, keeps us from vulnerable commitments to others, pushing us into lonely emptiness and isolation. Our certainty, reinforced through a thirst for psychic security, becomes rigid and judgmental, repressing life experience and fresh revelations that finally will devastate us. Our grandiosity, which begins simply as pride, habitually starts selling a story of ourselves that shades the truth and tolerates deceit, eventually leaving us exposed and desolate. Our control becomes obsessive, trampling the gifts of others even as life reveals the futility of our vain attempts at mastery. In all this, our growing self-deception blinds us to what is happening within.

We end up in devastating places where it feels as though our life is spinning out of control, that our emotions are no longer controlled by our gifted minds, and where we come face to face with the dread that accompanies the exposure of our illusions. This will happen to you, maybe in minor, repetitive incidents that gradually cripple you, or perhaps in a major crisis that results in the shaking of your foundations. Mystics call this internal crisis the dark night of the soul. Contemplatives like Thomas Merton speak of this crippling experience as the beginning of the annihilation of the false self. For those immersed in Christian scripture, the blinding intervention of Saul on the road to Damascus may come to mind.

The good news is that these are moments when you will have a choice. You can face into the blindness and pain, believing that light, somehow, will come. Or you can run and hide, still trying to cling to the false myths about yourself.

What will have prepared you for those critical moments, when self-surrender or self-protection hang in the balance, is that holding space. It will depend on whether you've developed this spiritual infrastructure, using the tools and practices available, to navigate the turbulent waters that now seem to engulf you.

Without a holding space to process these painful threats, you will be tempted to head back to home base in denial, digging yourself ever deeper into the false, separate self. But if you can find a way to be vulnerable and safe while the illusions of your life are exposed, you can take a leap of surrender in the face of these threats. Of course that will seem daunting, and nearly impossible, like facing into death. But if you can hold on and journey through this tunnel of annihilation, you'll discover your true self beginning to emerge, more real than anything you've known. You are embracing the image of God, residing at the core of your being.

Now you can let these self-made building blocks tumble before the grace-filled building blocks of the authentic self. The threats you face that seem impossible chasms can become a transformational bridge from the dross that's covered your life with ambition to something authentic, pure gold:

- out of the deepest emptiness and hiding, you begin to experience the thirst for community, learning to live as those whose lives are held in common by the love of God. This is the movement *from self-sufficiency to belonging*;

- out of the deconstruction of rational systems of security, you emerge. Here you nurture presence to the embedded spirituality of your life in God. Here you encounter in creation, art, and worship the movement *from certainty to connection*;
- out of despair over your deceit, you find the courage to start with who you actually are (not who you want to be, pretend to be, present yourself to be). Here you experience liberation from grandiosity, discovering who God has created and called you to be in the movement *from grandiosity to authenticity*; and
- out of your false belief that you can "handle this," you surrender to uncontrollable grace. Here you meet a generative hope in God's preferred and promised future not just for our personal agendas or pathways, but for the world, in the movement *from control to trust*.

Grace mysteriously erupts when you courageously face your pain. I've seen this happen in my life and in the journeys of those who have mentored and guided me. And this is what I know can become your reality, wherever you presently find yourself on your journey.

So, I invite you to imagine such a life. A life rich in belonging, a life filled with sacred connection, a life nurturing your authenticity, and a life brimming with indefatigable trust. Don't we all long for such a life? Wouldn't we do whatever we could to welcome this way of living?

Even more. Isn't this the only way to equip you for the long road ahead? Wouldn't this place you on that path which relentlessly and courageously pursues the transformation of this broken world into a glimpse of justice in the restored creation we yearn to see? If "the means are the end in the making," then isn't this our only way forward?

This trajectory for your soul's journey will beckon you to apprehend, beyond all else, that your very essence is created by God, holds God's image, and is rooted in the flow of this love. But this is never confined to isolated, inward, individual experience. God's presence and life can never be contained in that bounded, limited space. This love is boundless and always breaks the boundaries you may try to impose. When you see the image of God imprinted on your inner being, you are connected to all that God loves. That is what it means to affirm that the inward journey and the outward journey intrinsically are linked together, as one. When you discover your true self, beginning to emerge through layers of dross that are melting away, you are discovering your connection with, and embracing your participation in, the love that is ever moving to transform the world.

Grace mysteriously erupts when you courageously face your pain.

Your work and mine is to open our journeys to the flames of an eternal Love, consuming layers of dross and revealing the image of our Maker reflected back to a beloved world.

IV.

From Self-Sufficiency to Belonging

Holy Cross Abbey rests close to the Shenandoah River nearby Berryville, Virginia, sixty miles from the nation's capital. As a Trappist monastery, the community's life begins with Vigils at 3:30 AM, and its daily rhythm is framed by four other times of gathered prayer that punctuate the monks' work and rest. This eventually became a sacred physical place for me, nurturing my inward holding space while I worked on Capitol Hill.

The monastery experimented with a "retreatants in community" opportunity, inviting individuals to live in the monastery with the monks for longer periods of time. I took some time off work to do this. One afternoon I wandered into its library. A book, *Self-Analysis* by Karen Horney, caught my attention. In one chapter Horney describes various neurotic trends. One immediately penetrated my heart: neurotic self-sufficiency. Each line felt cut like psychological incisions through my defenses, defining my own neuroses as the

> necessity never to need anybody, or to yield to any influence, or to be tied down to anything, any closeness involving the danger of enslavement. Distance and separateness as the only source of

security; dread of needing others, of ties, of closeness, of love.

Self-sufficiency hides behind the masks of competence and achievement. Your ability to do things proficiently and well protects you from dependence on others, which may pose some deep and unacknowledged threats. Grasping the neurotic hold of self-sufficiency on your soul, however, is hindered by the culture's affirmation of these qualities.

Our society extols self-sufficiency. Dependence on others, especially among men, smacks of weakness. Injunctions urge us to "pull ourselves up by our own bootstraps." Conservative politicians decry those who become reliant on governmental assistance for their welfare, warning that this destroys their initiative and independent agency.

From its founding, American society has placed the highest value on the individual as the focus for identity. Individual rights are enshrined in our Constitution and embedded in shared assumptions about the purpose and fulfillment of life. It's our unquestioned starting point. All this, of course, reflects the heritage of liberal Western democracies. And the primacy of individual self-fulfillment has infected many strands of modern Western Christianity.

One of the treasures addressing self-sufficiency I discovered while wandering into the library of Holy Cross Abbey was a series of cassette tapes of talks given by Thomas Merton when he was at the Abbey of Our Lady of Gethsemani in Kentucky. In one talk he dissects the spiritual illusion of individuality and its effects:

> What blocks a direct relationship to God is the modern idea of . . . an autonomous self, separate from all else, individualistically trying to make the right decisions according to principles and ideology and logic, etc. That all blocks one's direct contact with God in life—in relationships with people in love. Life is impregnated with love at all levels. We must be open to it. That is how we find God's will. God's nature is to create love. Man's nature has indefinite possibilities for the growth of love.

Other cultures work from an assumption that relationships and community are foundational for understanding reality and human development. The African concept of Ubuntu, for instance, often shared by the late Bishop Desmond Tutu, has the core assumption that "a person is a person through other people." Relationships are the matrix for understanding our humanity. And Native American cultures also begin at a similar place. Andrea Sullivan-Clarke, a philosophy professor and member of the Wind Clan of the Muscogee Nation of Oklahoma, explains in a 2022 *New York Times* article that "many Indigenous communities consider the idea of 'person' as what it means to be born a member of a people."

With relationships at the center, the starting point is community.

But that's not my story, nor that of millions of others like me. Raised in a comfortable middle-class home by a loving family in a nearly all-white suburb of Chicago, my life was infused with unrecognized privilege. An ardent evangelical faith shaped my familial and social subculture, which fit like a glove with conservative Republican white nationalism. Individual freedom was priceless. I perceived self-sufficiency to be my virtuous starting point. Unconsciously this was a highly effective bulwark protecting my false self from the fear of entrapment. To me, an individualistic faith fused with personal achievement justified my comfortable, separated, protected self.

Whether your self-sufficiency becomes a neurotic obsession, rather than a healthy step away from crippling dependence, is affected by the circumstances shaping your life's journey. Larry Rasmussen, an author and friend, recast this whole discussion for me, once sharing: "In New York City I rode with a cab driver from India who exulted in the fact that in America he could truly be a self-sufficient individual whereas back home he would never escape belonging—belonging, in his case, to the Dalits." For some, self-sufficiency is a mark of liberation from social systems and economic forces holding them in oppression.

In the process of human development you are led from the physical and psychological dependence of childhood through the search for self-identity in adolescence to healthy independence and self-sufficiency as you enter adulthood. That's all part of needed ego maturity that weans you from the dependency of childhood and allows for your autonomous selfhood to emerge. But if that's how you describe your present psychological development, you haven't arrived yet at the final goal and ending point for your journey. Ironically, the development of necessary ego strength is the precursor to your capacity to seek pathways of self-giving in service and sacrifice for others, and to confront the wounds that halt your movement from the protected self to the surrendered self.

If your self-sufficiency forms a protective shell, it will inhibit your capacity to develop enriching, mutually dependent relationships with other individuals, colleagues, and groups. You can readily find examples, even while watching police dramas on TV. In one season of the PBS show *Unforgotten*, an outstanding detective, Jessica James, gets promoted to DCI within her unit of the British police. But her personal life is falling apart, and her husband, Steve, has told Jessica he's leaving her and the two boys. She's committed to succeeding in her new post, but her inner emotional depletion makes it difficult to establish connection with her new colleagues. Distraught, she comes home and her mom, there to watch the boys, joins her for a glass of wine in the kitchen:

> *Jess:* I just feel very weird. Cause this is not me. I don't do needy.
> *Mom:* People like to feel needed, Jess.
> *Jess:* Really?
> *Mom:* Yes, oddly they do. . . .
> *Jess:* What is your point?

Mom: All your life, Jess, even when you were little, you were always this person who could just cope with anything. So self-sufficient, unfazeable. But that's hard for people. For me and your dad sometimes. For your sister, definitely. Maybe it is for Steve.

In Karen Horney's description, the "dread of needing others, of ties, of closeness, of love" drives self-sufficiency as it seeks to bolster the protected self. Serial failed relationships, broken commitments, the undermining of community, and distancing by others wounded along the way are the results. Emptiness ensues, which is either avoided or repressed by self-destructive behaviors. For most, however, an underlying hunger "to know and be known" in relationships with others can't be completely quenched.

If your self-sufficiency forms a protective shell, it will inhibit your capacity to develop enriching, mutually dependent relationships with other individuals, colleagues, and groups.

If the dread of emotional entanglement and dependency drives you into withdrawal, it solves a short-term problem while inflaming a long-term need. If you can hear it, echoing within this self-imposed emptiness is the perennial question of whether you will move away from or toward your deepest longings for connection in authentic relationships. But given your capacity for rationalization to explain away recurrent turbulence in relationships with others, you may not be fully aware of what is at stake. With enough holding space, however, the truth will begin to seep in.

The Refiner's Fire Burns

To illustrate, in the years before my marriage to Kaarin, neurotic self-sufficiency inhibited any serious commitment to her or any woman and restrained my embrace of community. The refiner's fire burned hot throughout that time at the Holy Cross Abbey and beyond. The levels of my false self, revealed so clearly in Karen Horney's description, were progressively and relentlessly exposed and began to be burned away.

My often-unconscious drive had been to preserve a space of protected autonomy and freedom at all psychological costs. For those of us who desperately protect that autonomy, with work both spiritual and psychological we can often trace that desperate hold in us to it roots. In my experience the ways my mother's love felt possessive and smothering shifted something in me. While, as many children do, outwardly I sought to please her, inwardly I hungered for a space of my own.

In my early single life much of this got infused into my relationships with women, where my need for self-sufficiency got projected in damaging ways. So I ran from commitment, constantly. Preserving my autonomy was the driving force. Sexual intimacy produced guilt and then distance, protecting my self-sufficiency.

In the time at the Abbey, a combination of vivid dreams, readings from ancient mystics and contemporary psychologists, conversations with my monastic friend, Father Stephen, and silence while I waited for dawn, began to pull all these connections together. Seeing how my wounded, obsessive need for self-sufficiency had been sabotaging my quest for loving, intimate relationship felt devastating.

May 12, 1974, age 28

We each come face to face with our own utter helplessness, our utter selfishness, our own total dependence on God's love. . . . For me, that reveals my desire to keep independent from love, under the myth that I am everything I need to be unto myself. . . . It is through reducing me to that state of total weakness and brokenness where God's love can begin to seep into my life. That is how, in Merton's analogy, the wax gets soft so it can receive God's imprint.

Your self-sufficiency has probably been serving you well. It may have liberated you from immature dependency and fueled an inner drive that has propelled you forward in your career. If you are a leader, and an activist, you've found the independence needed to make courageous choices. But the neurotic temptation is to start believing in your own invincibility. You find a subtle pride in not really needing to rely on anyone else, and knowing your judgment and skill in what you do are the best. Your security becomes wedded to your self-sufficiency, and you develop defenses against relationships or commitments that threaten this.

I've known some enormously gifted leaders and pastors who kept themselves isolated and alone. At times that's understandable, and there can be a profound "loneliness at the top." Once I heard the NPR show "Freakonomics" discussing the number of CEOs of major corporations who report that they have no real friends. Yes, gifted leadership requires a certain prophetic detachment. But in many cases I've seen emotionally isolated, proudly self-sufficient leaders crippled and even destroyed, overwhelmed by their inner emptiness. That can take many forms—devastating sexual indiscretion, addictive substance abuse, or the abject refusal to accept the counsel of other colleagues—resulting in debilitating damage to an organization or congregation.

Author Debie Thomas describes the challenge this way: "It's hard in our self-promoting culture to confess that we are lost and lifeless on our own. That our glory lies in surrender, not self-sufficiency."

That's why it's essential to be attentive to the grip of self-sufficiency in how you live your life. And why it's essential to be willing to encounter the emptiness that it breeds and walk through this as a bridge to belonging. Most likely that journey will lead you through three primary relationships: with a partner or spouse in a covenanted commitment (should this be your calling); with a community of close, mutual relationships; and with God, not as an idea, but as a living presence of your deepest belonging.

A Crucible of Emptiness and Love

The thirty-five-day monastic retreat described earlier, where I was confronted by my neurotic self-sufficiency, came after visiting Kaarin for two weeks in Japan. We had broken off our relationship two years earlier. Now we embraced our commitment to be married. But entering this monastic bubble, protected from society's external encroachments, opened internal territory of my life to psychological dissection and spiritual discovery. Our wedding was planned for August, and Kaarin was still in Japan. Yet I felt desperate in what was being revealed of my life and knew I was trying to survive in anxious, liminal space.

The compass of my inward journey searched for signs of God's presence amid interior emptiness. Almost simultaneously, I was directed toward my love for Kaarin even in the face of a crippling anxiety, punctuated by bursts of bountiful bliss. I came to see the roots of my paralyzing emotional wounds that had previously left my commitment to Kaarin in ruins. God's love uncontrollably broke through my faltering defenses and occasionally reached my heart and soul.

The fire burned in so many ways.

> MAY 11, 1974
> *After 72 hours of intense psychological and spiritual work, I was out walking in the fields, even singing spontaneous verses to the tune of chants repeated daily. . . . Prayer*

flowed for Kaarin; I sensed the closest communion and union. . . .

I was about to go back, but suddenly, on my knees, prayed, "Lord Jesus I love you." The words surged forth with tears flowing from my eyes. And then I quieted even that prayer, just to be in this Love. . . .

All creation, all life is changed in these moments. Every person becomes loved—seen as a gift—seen in their true Reality.

Only my inner, contemplative journey could break the imprisoning hold of my neurotic self-sufficiency. Initially, of course, I had no understanding of this. But the contemplative journey brought the experiences of a Love—God's love—that intersected my inner self at a depth of emotional, psychological, and spiritual reality. I came to discover that this Love was the most real, was Life itself. And it was the only way to unlock within me any capacity to love that was free—not rooted in my abilities or driven by my needs.

May 2, 1974
"Purity of the heart is to will one thing," wrote Kierkegaard.

Only when God is sought in such utter poverty of spirit can God impart to us the love of God's own life—that love that has no need, other than to give itself away to another.

MAY 17, 1974
We are meant to turn desire into love. That is what life is for.

Analyzing the Inner Journey

Your story of how self-sufficiency seeks to possess your life and circumscribe your relationships may be very different from mine. But it's likely to have roots in your relationship with your father, mother, or other primary figure in your life when you were young. It's worth exploring those dynamics. Sometimes, despite the pain of the process, what emerges out of the refiner's fire is pure gold.

In my case, my inward contemplative journey began unlocking my capacity to love, and to make progress on the journey from self-sufficiency to belonging. Revelatory moments were decisive, like those experienced at the abbey in the rolling fields near Berryville. Yet, for you or for me, the process of this journey is measured not by weeks, but by years. Fourteen years after that monastic retreat I dove into sessions of psychological therapy while living in Missoula, Montana. That provided a holding space where I could be vulnerable and safe while I delved more deeply into the roots of my neurotic self-sufficiency first identified at Berryville, as well as the dynamics of my relationships with others in my ongoing journey.

Among the things I discovered at age forty-three were these:

June 16, 1988

My mother's deep identification with me—with those parts of me that pleased her, that excelled, that achieved, that did things right, that provided an extension of her identity—built a strong pattern of intuiting what would please her, and what would not. So, my energy and identity responded around this learned desire and pattern to achieve my sense of self-worth through fulfilling her expectations, which became my expectations.

But in that process, the sense of who I was separate from her—who I was in my own self, in my own real autonomy—was clouded, hidden, and nearly lost. . . .

This pattern seems clear. I've often been willing to serve emotionally as a tool for others, to help them succeed and thus have them pleased with me. The relationship with Senator Mark Hatfield is an example. He had an indirectness in his style. I could anticipate what he wanted to say and do. Some say no one else was like me in that position with him. Probably so. And a strong attachment was there. Yet, I left working with him in large part to be my own person, to not be in his shadow, to not lose myself, and to live my own life.

This seems to be a constant theme and struggle—to find my true identity, to express my own journey, to be rooted in a sense of selfhood. . . .

The contemplative style of spirituality appealed so strongly to me because it provided that space which I needed for my true self to emerge.

I began seeing my story and writing it as I journaled. You would tell a different story with different central characters and struggles. How *would* you tell your story? Those studying Karen Horney's work seek to clarify what pushes a trait, such as self-sufficiency, into neurosis, that is, when self-sufficiency becomes compulsive, in a sense seizing and defining the whole person. Even beginning by asking whether your drive for self-sufficiency feels inwardly like a default system automatically kicking in whenever mutuality and vulnerable commitments pose threats is helpful, helping you explore what is at play in your life and psyche.

Yes, it will take work on your part to discover the sources and reasons for those threats. You may be living in reaction to a fiercely domineering father, compelled to protect your own self-directed sense of agency. Or you may have been deeply traumatized by one or more persons who seriously abused the power they held over you, and the trust you gave them. But whatever your life's circumstance, take the time to also consider this: With whom and in which places do you have safe space to look with honesty at the painful cracks in your facade as you seek to uncover the gold of your essence?

Encountering Emptiness

The same contemplative journey providing me a holding space that was set apart also yielded painful revelations into how my self-sufficiency subtly protected my separated self from serious commitment to forms of community with others, inhibiting true belonging. What I discovered and named was, frankly, unlovely: my pretension, my judgment of others, and my self-importance, all with a self-centeredness fostered in the petri dish of praise from others as I constantly sought to feed off their approval of my external self.

From the first hesitant days of my inward journey nurtured at Church of the Saviour, and in the earliest entries in my journal, a dim light still shone on my deficit. At twenty-four I wrote:

> AUGUST 10, 1969
> *The tendency now is to continually view myself as the center of conversation, etc. There's not much humility. And I remain quite critical, unjustly so, of others. I'm not truly loving, not following Christ's life. I must be less aloof and arrogant—and truly be a humble, loving follower of my Lord.*

Beckoned but threatened by belonging to a close community, I decided to join one of Church of the Saviour's mission groups, with weekly meetings, intentional accountability to spiritual disciplines, and shared commitment to a common mission. In my journey this is where I first began to learn and experience the call to community as distinct from simply "joining" a church. But attempting to embrace life in Christian community often revealed my emptiness, and the pervasiveness of my self-sufficiency. After reading Bonhoeffer's *Life Together* in a Church of the Saviour class, about barriers to community in each of our lives, I wrote:

> FEBRUARY 4, 1970, AGE 24
> *My problem—the feeling of superiority, which makes me want not to tolerate many others within the group, and only love those who are like me. If someone seems so obviously insecure, or not intellectual, or in some other way annoying to me, I feel they are an imposition and find it hard to tolerate them, much less love them.*

Be forewarned. Your movement from self-sufficiency to belonging is likely to first lead to an encounter with your emptiness borne of the futility of clinging to your own separateness as the foundation of security. The process moves step by step, with steps not always in the right direction. This is no neat, linear, sequential process. Usually, it's more cyclical, yet you grow in the capacity to trust more in belonging than in your own autonomy.

Hinge points in your journey will arise as you respond to the inner promptings your holding space has uncovered. Choices are required. Sometimes they are simple choices moving you in a different direction. Or they may be dramatic, borne from moments of conversion when one sobs on a lonely beach in utter anguish over a sense that life has you trapped, chained to a sense of reality that isn't reality. But those who stay with the work always move out of emptiness, despair, even annihilation. Your movement from self-sufficiency to belonging, though, is likely to traverse through portals of pain.

Intentional choices to move from self-sufficiency to belonging are not just intellectual or theological decisions.

Rather, you learn to abandon yourself and take a "leap of faith" into the hope that grace and love will liberate your protected self into the gift of vulnerable relationships with others.

Those choices in my journey gradually began to interrupt the normalcy of my abnormal, hectic, crusading, depleting, self-absorbed lifestyle. Over time, I chose to join with friends in starting a commune, taking a journaling class, embarking on an unplanned retreat to an unknown monastery, making a membership commitment to Church of the Saviour, flying to Japan to discover love with Kaarin, being part of the newly formed Sojourners community, leaving all my life in DC behind for healing hospitality in Missoula, Montana, completing the process for becoming an ordained minister, embracing an ecumenical calling in Geneva, finding a spiritual director from the Grandchamp community in Switzerland, and so much more. Journeys open up from that intentionality and reflection.

Some of these choices were agonizing, threatening, and full of risk as well as promise. But each was an interruption, breaking through the protective, restraining canopy of my self-referential life and creating a potential holding space to process pain and grace.

Belonging to God

At the core of your journey from self-sufficiency through emptiness to belonging is the discovery and continual rediscovery that you belong to God. That bedrock of belonging weaves through your commitment, if part of your life's calling, to a covenanted life partner and to your life together with sisters and brothers in community. Yet it has a solitary locus that then flows forth in bonds of belonging to others, touching a love that knows only how to give itself away. Radical dependence on God is detachment from all else—but then it is love for all else.

The underlying purpose for you to construct a holding space is creating an interior place where encountering God's presence and love becomes a possibility. This has little or nothing to do with what you "believe." One of the problems of many inherited, Western forms of Christianity is their being founded on a belief in beliefs, the rational appropriation of mental and theological constructs. But I expect what you truly hunger and thirst for is an encounter with God's presence that reaches your soul. That's what holds the potential for ongoing, inward transformation rooting your outward journey in a reality transcending immediate circumstances and oppressive obstacles.

Radical dependence on God is detachment from all else—but then it is love for all else.

Perhaps your journey is similar to mine. The pietistic, individualistic spirituality of my evangelical upbringing proved incapable in providing tools for an authentic inward journey. They no longer revealed God's presence. Rather, they seemed to obscure it. That's why, at least in my case, I was led to the discovery of fresh tools, practices, people, and language that awakened God's presence, in periodic epiphanies, at the core of my being.

No matter if your journey has similarities to or differences from mine, you can develop the holding space to open your attentiveness to ways the mysterious intersection of God's presence might touch your inner life. That may happen in ways or at places seen as wholly unpredictable, or perhaps in traditional vehicles of the church designed originally as carriers of embodied, sacramental grace. But always it will come as an unexpected surprise, far beyond your ability to predict, manipulate, or control.

In such seemingly transfigured moments, you are likely to experience dross being consumed as your true self is being revealed and refined. In that process the call to you is simply this: to say, with all your being, "I am here now." To be present to this Presence.

You may remember glimmers of such moments saturated with grace even from your childhood, or at other points in the journey. Perhaps they were shrouded in the debris of spiritual practices long discarded, or else forgotten as the protective layers of your false self were reconstructed with its concealing, repressive facade. But even if effectively hidden and covered, that Presence is never extinguished. It continues to flicker beneath the consciousness, waiting for those moments when cracks will let in light.

James Finley, in his memoir *The Healing Path*, calls these moments "graced awakenings." He shares his early experience of God's permeating Presence in a pig barn at the Abbey of Gethsemani. It was like the embracing, mystical experience

Thomas Merton had at the corner of Fourth and Walnut in Louisville, Kentucky. Finley writes:

> So it is that we in the graced moments of our awakening, are rendered utterly vulnerable in realizing we are powerless to diminish how invincibly precious we are in God's eyes in the midst of our wayward ways. So it is that we, in our graced moments of awakening, are momentarily silenced in realizing ourselves to be ineffably absorbed in the presence of God, beyond what words can say.

These graced awakenings that can be hinge points of your journey and are not reserved for just a few rarified "mystics." They are available to you, to me, to each of us. Every person carries deep within the image of God, like gold, waiting to be revealed and refined. Not all of us are given the gift to write and interpret the inner dynamics of this process, but we all are given the opportunity to experience it. Again, Finley writes,

> Little did I know that as I learned to gaze into the secret of God's face, I would discover it to be like a mirror, reflecting back to me who God eternally knows and calls me to be in the midst of all that remained unresolved in my mind and heart.

In my own wayward journey my fragile holding space first had to allow me to face the way my self-sufficiency bred and concealed a deep inner loneliness and dread. Until those cracks were revealed, God's love was deflected away, rather than reflected back. Gordon Cosby, founder of Church of the Saviour, became my spiritual director. And often, as I listened to his preached word, it cut through to me:

JULY 31, 1972, AGE 27
My response to a sermon by Gordon Cosby on love—the need to experience this inwardly. "He who loves is born of God" (1 John).

It means facing the dread of one's loneliness, one's nothingness, one's sinfulness, one's alienation. It means living into this dread—confronting it and dealing directly with it. And then, purely through grace, it means allowing God's love to . . . become the answer to those needs, to the state of one's estrangement. It means being dependent upon nothing other than this love.

Surveying your journey, I expect you'll find a scattering of miscellaneous circumstances and happenings that, in retrospect, are not miscellaneous at all, but providential points on your way to an unexpected, graced awakening. That may describe your present path. If so, avoid predicting or planning. Just take the next step forward.

The graced awakening that formed the rest of my life came from an unplanned, spontaneously arranged retreat to the Holy Cross Monastery, a place I'd never been. The days were cold, gray, and misty; my soul was depleted. Yet fresh tools and practices from the previous three years had constructed enough of a holding space for something to happen.

> December 15, 1972, age 27
>
> *These are the experiences I want to recount today, at Holy Cross Monastery. Following the afternoon service, I remained in the chapel. And as I prayed, I felt a spontaneous flowing of joyous adoration, from the heart, from that same root of experience—the same kind of apprehension; it was prompted from the deep within me and was simply a sense of love and warmth for Christ. "Christ, I love you." The Jesus prayer, which I had been repeating that morning, suddenly flowed out naturally. I simply let myself revel and dwell in this deep expression of praise; it was not just a feeling or emotion—not just that. Rather, I felt—or intuited—that it was a response of my soul, of my whole self, toward Christ, and his love.*
>
> *As I pondered that love and this experience, I then thought of those closest to me—first my family . . . —I felt as deep a love for them as I ever have. . . .*
>
> *And as I prayed for the members of my group—and for people in the office—much of the same type of experience occurred; I felt deep love and concern, and I saw them for what they could be; saw them through the eyes of Christ's love—saw them as being loved.*
>
> *It was as though I was caught up in the force of this love. . . .*
>
> *On the walk that afternoon, as I looked at the trees through the mist, and the gray sky beyond it, all covered by*

a soft, slight rainy air, I gazed, and I sensed that there was a deeper reality behind this all—but a reality that was also present in the creation. I watched my breath condense into small bits of clouds; yes—a deeper reality beyond this, yet present in it; transcendent, yet still immanent; involved in the created, visible, sensual order of things—yet transcendent from it—not bound by it; rather upholding it.

Over five decades have passed since those moments, decades filled with times of agony, and also rich joy. But those days at Berryville are seared in my soul's memory. They became the most important hinge point in my journey, prompted by a leap of faith, and setting the trajectory for all that has followed. It was from those days that I became certain, not in my head, but at the inner center of my being, that I belonged to God.

As my hair grays and my steps slow, a few certainties like this remain, held mostly in my heart. I can't pass them on to you, though I wish I could. But I can invite you on the path. Whether you are twenty-two or seventy-two, that path awaits. What I do know is that it will lead you, in unexpected ways, to graced awakenings.

Belonging as the Starting Point

The holding space I began creating in those early years of my young-adult, inward journey let enough light in with the experience at Berryville and many more that followed.

Eventually belonging rather than self-sufficiency became my more frequent starting point. Further, community became the core definition of belonging to any church, and of any attempt to create a fresh expression for embodying the call to be God's gathered people. This commitment to community has been shared by Kaarin, who, though on her own journey, met me on mine. Subsequently, in each location where Kaarin and I put down roots, we've sought or started a group in the life of a church where our belonging would be tangible, vulnerable, and accountable. On some occasions this crashed with wounding pain. Often, it flourished.

The movement you make from self-sufficiency into emptiness and then to belonging will show up in slow but clear shifts in the default dispositions of your heart. Psychological responses are altered. The late Father Thomas Keating explained how centering prayer works to influence that process. Through periodic conversations with him, reading his books, and while on annual retreats at St. Benedict's Monastery, I gained a deeper understanding of how my inner journey gradually was transforming my emotional wiring. Belonging in communities of vulnerable relationships and in the intimate embrace of God's love became comfort to me. Keating explained these psychological and spiritual dynamics in these ways, which I want to share with you:

> OCTOBER 26, 2006, AGE 61
> *Keating traces the evolution of the "human condition" in an involved analysis of psycho-social development and human evolution. The core insight is that we are*

programmed early on to self-defeating patterns of behavior in part resulting because the sense of "self" is fully developed in present (Western) civilization without the necessary corresponding union of the self to God, and thus all the various forms of self-centeredness keep humans from a satisfying happiness. . . .

My needs of self-aggrandizement, my neurotic self-sufficiency, my fears of commitment, my desire for self-centered gratification—it is fair to say that all these were rooted in a lack of basic physical nurture and an emphasis on acceptance through what I could achieve.

The challenge, Keating is saying, is to allow one's spiritual journey to undo the false emotional systems ("energy centers") that get one stuck with excessive demands that are ultimately self-defeating. So, the key is one's journey spiritually toward "resting in God." The process of centering prayer allows for these "demands" to be diminished and these "energy centers" dry up and are deprived of their power.

This really is not that different from what I have thought about in the past, but it seems deeper, and more integrated.

Keating says, "The spiritual journey is not a success story but the ever-increasing knowledge of our self-centeredness."

As you continue on this inward journey, you will notice how your default responses begin to change. In times of crisis, anxiety, and pain, instead of falling backward into protective isolation, you fall forward into vulnerable, loving bonds of belonging. Courageous choices evolve into reliable habits. And these endure, shaping the contours of your ongoing pilgrimage toward the surrendered self.

Surrendering our protected self to holy bonds of belonging is a life-long invitation from the One who created us to belong. We cling to the myths of self-sufficiency that defend our separated, false self until, in emptiness and openness, we discover embrace at our core by the love of God, from which nothing can separate us.

Once we live in this embrace in our soul, at the center of our life, our relationship to the world and to all creation is transformed. This love, from which we can never be separated, cannot be separated from the world pain, suffering, and injustice. It draws us to confront the cruelty, callousness, and brokenness of the world's systems because this is the love that has sacrificed itself to overcome the power of evil and redeem the world.

Our thirst for justice can only be sustained if we draw on the wellspring of this love, becoming embedded in the depths of our being. When this love burns away the dross of our lives and uncovers God's image, reflected back, it reveals that image of God at the heart of every person. That is the ultimate foundation for countering the realities of racial oppression, income inequality, voter suppression, LGBTQ and transgender discrimination, gender bias, white supremacy, sexual exploitation, immigrant persecution, disability discrimination, and more. This same boundless love connects us intrinsically and humbly to the whole of creation, as the foundation for all efforts to build climate justice and protect the diversity and flourishing of all life. And it rests at the heart of all peacemaking, reverberating in the revolutionary appeal to love one's enemies.

The movement from self-sufficiency to belonging relinquishes the core of our being to the boundless generosity of God's love in places wherever that love is present. It results in the deepest possible solidarity with the world as it suffers in pain, but is sustained by grace. Living into this reality is the soulwork of justice.

V.

From Certainty to Connection

When the pictures of the cosmos from the Webb telescope first appeared, I was enthralled. They mystified me, inviting an awe beyond my comprehension. I wanted to understand more and grasp what I was seeing.

One evening an astronomer and friend in Santa Fe, Ed Barker, gave a presentation to our small fellowship group, Bread for the Journey, about the Webb telescope discoveries. Formerly Ed worked with the McDonald Observatory in Texas and collaborated with NASA on various projects. While he spoke clearly, the implications all seemed to bend rationality and defy the boundaries of linear explanation. Even as he laid out facts, they seemed to melt into inexplicable wonder. When I tried to decipher more of what the Webb telescope's astonishing pictures were portraying, I ended up with descriptions of perplexities that left my mind numb.

These pictures, we're told, are of a galaxy from forty million years ago.

The galaxy we think we know and get a glimpse of is called the Milky Way. As a child I used to look at the stars, finding the Big Dipper, the Little Dipper, and then was told that I could "see" the Milky Way. But now I've learned that the Milky Way, our galactical home, has between 100 and

400 billion stars. Yes, *billion.* And each star has at least one planet, or more. So there are perhaps between one and ten trillion planets just in the Milky Way. We here on Planet Earth have "discovered" a mere 5,502 planets beyond those in our solar system.

But that's one galaxy. So, I wondered, how many galaxies are there? The answer is thought to be between two-hundred-billion and one-trillion galaxies. And the typical galaxy has 100 billion stars. Some, like the Milky Way, have more. It's impossible to conceive of these numbers. But, Ed explained, think of it this way: There are more stars in the universe—at least two trillion—than there are grains of sand on all the beaches found on Planet Earth.

This universe, in which the earth finds its home, cannot even be imagined. Trying to do so in any case would be fruitless. That's because the unfathomable features of the universe compose only a fraction—maybe 5 percent—of the whole. The remaining 95 percent is made up of dark matter and dark energy, which are unknown and unobservable to even the most advanced telescopes, like the Webb. We don't know what we don't know.

The creeds of the church begin by proclaiming God as Creator of the heavens and earth, echoing the first chapter of Genesis. The writers, however, had no idea what they were asserting. Their view of the "heavens" held in a dome covering the earth was comprehensible, if completely deluded. When I try to absorb the indescribable descriptions of the infinite extent and age of the universe, I ask, "Where is God?" And, "Who is God?"

The New Testament makes this all even more perplexing when John, describing the incarnation of Jesus Christ, asserts that "all things came into being through him" (Jn 1:3). Colossians goes further, declaring "in him all things hold together" (Col 1:17). But what can it possibly mean, rationally, for a thirteen-billion-year-old universe, with billions of galaxies and stars exceeding all the grains of sand on the earth to be held together and function according to the second person of the Trinity affirmed by one religion of one tiny planet out of trillions? That's beyond comprehension.

Christian faith is rooted in the astonishing conviction that the Creator of all that is, beyond our knowing, including all the dark energy and matter, somehow became fully present in the womb of a Jewish peasant girl in Palestine two thousand years ago on this planetary speck of the cosmos. I conclude that Christianity is an irrational religion. If I needed any further convincing of this, the Webb telescope does the work. Its pictures, while promoting awe, destroy our certainty and show us as specks on a canvas that seems unending.

For much of my journey I've depended on a rational framework for holding my faith. Of course, it changed and evolved. But I could fall back on a reasonable, theological way of knowing what I believed and why. Yes, it was called faith. But it really was mostly belief, which is far different. Then, as pillars of rational certainty began to deteriorate, eventually they crumbled. Most recently, these revelations about the universe accelerated that process. I can understand why Stephen Hawking said he was an atheist.

Your journey may be far different. Perhaps like many people, revelations about the universe from astronomy's advances inspire convictions about God's power, majesty, and grandeur. I have no desire to dissuade you of those responses. But I do believe that at some point in your journey, whether from academic study, or personal tragedy, or foreign travel, or intercultural dialogue, or simply courageous curiosity, your system of rational certainty about God, faith, and life's meaning is likely to deteriorate and eventually crumble. You'll want to gather your beliefs and defenses, but don't. Let what needs to crumble, crumble. Instead, turn your attention to where your attention seems to go, and to what happens next.

Losing Belief in Beliefs

The most enduring foundations of your spiritual journey will emerge after your rational certainty of beliefs gets annihilated. Clinging to rational certainty, in fact, keeps your soul frozen and imprisoned. Estelle Frankel, in *The Wisdom of Not Knowing,* puts it this way: "One of the first lessons we all must learn in order to be free is how to 'bear' uncertainty and trust in the unknown." But this brings you first to experiences of bewilderment. You have biblical company in that journey. Think of the story of Jonah, for instance. Swallowed by a whale and then sent reluctantly on a preaching mission he desperately resisted, he retreated up a mountain, certain of what God would do to Nineveh. When nothing happens based on his firmly held "rational" expectations, he's distraught, in utter perplexity.

Or consider Mary, the mother of Jesus. Everything she understood about her life, her religion, and her forthcoming marriage is radically deconstructed by a vision and visitation from an angel. When Luke writes in his Gospel that she was "pondering these things in her heart," that is not some pious attribute but rather a frank description of how she was struggling to make sense out of all this in the face of her pervasive uncertainty.

Biblical examples like this are numerous. They illuminate the difference between *belief* and *faith*. Belief provides consent to rational propositions. Faith connects us to transcendence. Rabbi Joshua Heschel explains in his book *Who Is Man?* that "knowledge is fostered by curiosity; wisdom is fostered by awe. Awe precedes faith."

The award-winning movie *Conclave* provides a powerful sermon about certainty, doubt, and faith. The storyline follows a pope who has died and the cardinals who gather in their secluded conclave to select a successor. Rivalries, ecclesiastical politics, and questions about the church's future direction ensue. At the outset and into the heart of the drama, Cardinal Lawrence, dean of the College of Cardinals, delivers a homily to his fellow cardinals: "There is one sin I have come to fear above all else: certainty. If there was only certainty and no doubt, there would be no mystery, and therefore no need for faith."

When you're riveted to rational certainty as the way to ground your understanding of God, solidifying security about your actions and your life's purpose, you gravitate toward binary thinking. That means viewing life through a lens that differentiates clear either/or categories. *This is true, so that is false. This is good, so that is evil. This is right, so that is wrong.* And that binary thinking extends to perceptions of the world. *This is spiritual, and that is material. This is objective, and that is subjective. This is reality, and that is illusion.* Your brain is programmed in Western culture to think in this manner. It's how you make sense out of things, and how you make choices. To speak philosophically, this means seeing reality and history through a dialectic of opposing forces.

Binary thinking plays a useful role in your life. Literally, it moves you beyond doubt and preserves a sanctuary of rational certainty. Those who are activists, leaders, effective managers—those who really want to see things get done—will be attracted to binary thinking. In social and political life you will drive momentum for change by articulating what is right and what is wrong, which is the correct path forward and which is the mistaken one.

Yet that leads to also dividing people into binary categories. If you're narcissistic, you will quickly decide who is with you and who is against you. Your evaluation of others, and your personal relationships, can easily get driven by who is part of the tribe working for the changes you feel are imperative, and who is opposed. It's us and them. Of course, our political culture and our siloed news media thrive on constant binary thinking.

Your experience of God and your life as a follower of Jesus get shrunk and calcified when you're dependent on the rational certainty provided by such a framework. Wonder and mystery evaporate. Discernment gets blocked. Spiritual exploration is quashed. You'll find, I believe, that the active presence of Holy Spirit in your life, and your perception of the Spirit's work in the world, are seriously inhibited by the predictable certainty afforded by binary thinking.

So what happens when life's messiness disrupts your comfortable dependence on rational certainty? You'll feel disoriented, as though you're lost at sea. You won't be certain where to turn or whom to trust. If you have been shaped and transformed by pietistic beliefs, you may find that the authors and theologians who previously provided you intellectual clarity now leave you with more questions than answers. And the pietistic habits that previously sustained your spiritual life may now leave you feeling dry and hollow.

You're not alone. *Faith deconstruction* has become a popular term for describing what happens when a closed system of beliefs, often held from childhood, begin to disintegrate under skeptical examination, whether due to the moral hypocrisy of leaders or because of psychological trauma. Those on a self-declared journey out of the theological confines and tribal culture of white evangelicalism or traditional Catholicism, both of which have spawned a mini-industry of podcasts, books, speakers, and so on, meet an invitation to something deeper, truer, and not based on rationality or binary tropes.

Your bulwark of rational certainty undergirding your religious commitments may have been shaped by other forms of binary thinking. When the Protestant Reformers rejected the authoritarian absolutism and pervasive corruption of the Catholic Church in a historic deconstructing movement, their response to the vacuum of authority they created was to construct rationally persuasive systems of theological beliefs. Often they were written in purposefully binary ways, declaring what theological propositions were affirmed as true, and therefore what opposing propositions were condemned as false. All this was designed to erect an edifice of rational certainty for defining and protecting one's religious identity.

The problem, of course, is that the deconstructing impulse formed another construction for binding, rational purity. You may be one whose religious commitment has been solidified by such a framework, which answered your theological questions and provided intellectual certainty and security. Until it didn't.

Your reliance on rational certainty to solidify your religious convictions may be rooted in one of various Christian traditions. What they all have in common, however, is the heritage of Western Christianity, shaped in the context of the Enlightenment, over the past five centuries or so. Richard Rohr, reflecting on the wisdom of Teresa of Avila, summarizes the results of this legacy well:

> A terrible lust for certitude and rigid social order has characterized the last five hundred years of Western Christianity, and it has simply not served the soul well at all. Once we lost a spirituality of darkness as its own kind of light, there just wasn't much room for growth in faith, hope, and love.

For Catholics, that longing for certitude found expression in papal infallibility and hierarchical authority. For some whose understanding of the church and authority was transformed by the Protestant Reformation, words from the pulpit, confessions, and texts became truth, instead of the Word becoming flesh. For many evangelicals this "lust for certitude" found expression in airtight doctrines of biblical inerrancy, a "tightening of the screws."

For some of us, rational certainty about faith may have been annihilated by the moral inconsistencies of the church and its leaders rather than the intellectual inconsistencies of its belief systems. Tragic stories of hypocrisy, failure, and psychological destructiveness flow across denominational lines, filling podcasts and generating devastating headlines. Sexual abuse and its coverup in the Catholic Church have been revealed in the heartbreaking witness of the wounded, causing hundreds of thousands to leave the church, and often leave behind the earlier certainty of their faith.

The headline-grabbing scandals in Protestantism have often come from the public moral and spiritual disintegration of prominent leaders. Exposés, like *The Secrets of Hillsong* on Hulu, describe how a charismatic pastor like Carl Lentz descended into a publicized sexual scandal in a toxic organizational culture with no moral accountability. Or *Shiny Happy People: Duggar Family Secrets* on Amazon Prime, revealing the internal wounds, alienation, and disillusionment within the story of the fundamentalist family. Or the podcast *The Rise and Fall of Mars Hill*, chronicling how Marc Driscoll's toxic leadership style with its masculine authoritarianism, led to the collapse of the fifteen-thousand-member megachurch.

These are just three well-known stories that have been repeated countless times. The real victims are the tens of thousands whose certainty about their Christian beliefs was riveted to their expression within such congregations and organizations. You probably know folks like this, whose security about what they believed was annihilated by the hypocrisy that they perceived. This may have been also part of your journey.

Whatever the cause, when you reach the point in your journey where your prior rational certainty about God and your convictions about faith feel annihilated, you have entered a hinge point in your life's journey. How you respond will be decisive for your future.

Perhaps you will remain present and open to what you may discover, even as you feel engulfed by doubt and bewilderment. Perhaps you will retreat into the protective, psychological security of belief systems that have failed to ground your soul.

Estelle Frankel likens this to the experience of the Israelites wandering in the wilderness. Freed from their enslavement in Egypt, their freedom now confronted them with daily uncertainty, unpredictability, and a bewildering search for identity. Many questioned and doubted their God, even longing for the previous security of their oppression in Egypt. The challenge for them, and for you and me, was how to bear uncertainty. Manna became the symbolic vehicle for holding uncertainty. Each day enough manna was present, but only for that day. The journey was built day by day, as lessons of trust replaced certainty. The Israelites were given provision rather than answers. The wilderness became a sacred space to connect with God's mysterious presence. These patient practices of depending on daily bread prepared them, eventually, to cross the Jordan and enter a new land.

> *When you reach the point in your journey where your prior rational certainty about God and your convictions about faith feel annihilated, you have entered a hinge point in your life's journey. How you respond will be decisive for your future.*

Faith after Doubt

If you're at the point where your prior rational certainty is being deconstructed, patient dependence on daily bread sustains your journey. You may be consoled by these words of St. Augustine: "Doubt is but another element of faith." But you're at this precarious point in your soul's progress where you will need to cross a bridge into a place of deeper connection to God's presence. Doing so, however, requires you to walk through experiences of annihilation and bewilderment.

John Sanford, episcopal priest and Jungian psychotherapist, explains this well in *Mystical Christianity,* his commentary on the Gospel of John:

> As every psychotherapist knows, no new development can take place in people who are satisfied with themselves the way they are, or who do not doubt themselves, or whose belief systems about themselves and life is heavily entrenched. Such people suffer from what the Bible calls "hardening of the heart." . . . When we come to doubt ourselves, when our previous system of beliefs and previous ways of coping with life are threatened or shattered, we find ourselves in a crisis. Then we no longer know who we are or where we are going or what our purpose is. It is the crisis of meaning, and people who are plunged into it often find themselves in the midst of great darkness and disorientation.

The first temptation in this great darkness is to resist or to construct another system of rational certainty meant to be even more impregnable than the one that has crumbled. If you do so, you will miss the most important learning that can come from your crisis of meaning. The point isn't to correct the defects of your prior rational belief system. It is to be weaned away from your belief in beliefs as the way to obtain the certainty you desire. You are being invited into a different way of knowing, one found more in connectional experiences than in intellectual excursions.

In my spiritual journey I recall how I first began to internalize the difference between the intellectual knowledge of religious truths and the inward embrace of spiritual realities that provided a different pathway to truth. I knew in my mind what I believed about living a life in the presence of God's love, rationalized through a set of doctrinal assertions. But that wasn't *how* I needed to know. Here's what came to me then and remains with me now:

> JUNE 21, 1974, AGE 29
> *These transcendent truths make their impression, through the impulse of the Spirit, again and again. Spiritually they must be known, not intellectually; they must be apprehended through the knowledge of one's inward life in Christ.*
>
> *That is why simply knowing them intellectually is not real knowledge of them; that is why simply realizing them once and then recording it in the mind, is far from grasping this Truth.*
>
> *. . . The mind can reflect and record, but the heart grasps these truths, over and over, as Life.*

This is not to discredit the gift of intellectual pursuits or set up some false and simplistic dichotomy between the head and the heart. The mind, of course, is essential to the process of discovering realities that can ground your life and shape your actions. But our modern culture, shaped by the Enlightenment, has *elevated* rational thought as the exclusive avenue to truth. Then it has *isolated* rationality from the emotive, psychological, and spiritual dimensions of human life. You don't even need theology to grasp the superficiality of this approach to knowing truth. Numerous philosophers and phenomenologists have underscored the complex interrelationships among rational thought, subjective experience, and emotive realities.

Discovering Experiences of Connection

When your rational certainty breaks down—as of course it will—give attention to where your soul, the integrated center of your being, wanders. Where are you drawn? What do you long for? What gives you joy? What captures your curiosity? My guess is that you will be drawn to beckoning experiences of connection. You will gravitate toward places, persons, and practices where you discover emotional and spiritual forms of connectedness that resonate with your inner self. These will likely include connections not only to people, but to the created world where experiences of awe and transcendence intersect with you in worship, music, art, and practices that unlock a fresh spiritual encounter opening your inner self to God's presence.

Those who are called mystics nearly always display an intimate sense of connection to the created world. Often this comes with striking particularity, like a reflection on a stone, or Julian of Norwich's vision of a hazelnut. Because mystics grasp the interconnection of all things, they perceive God's presence as comingled with all creation. Contemplation radicalizes the sense of God's presence in the world.

The starting point for this connection comes in the concrete immediacy of life as it is encountered in creation and community, with its awe, its pain, and its suffering. This is never a flight from the world, which is a misguided stereotype of true mystics. Rather, it is the deepest embrace of the world. This provides the sustaining, irreplaceable heart of your commitment to justice. It doesn't depend on an abstract, intellectual ideology but on the concrete interconnection of your soul to the daily, devastating brokenness of the world, to the sacred giftedness that rests at creation's core, and the longing embrace of it all by God. Moving from the comfort of rational certainty to the mystery of sacred connection, this is how a radical commitment for the long term will well up from within your deepest self.

But you don't have to be Julian of Norwich or Thomas Merton to participate in this understanding of interconnectedness. The doorways that open the pathway of this experience will vary according to your life's setting and history. But in the shroud of intellectual uncertainty and doubt, you are likely to be drawn to experiences with nature that inspire transcendent awe. It's a sign that your soul is searching for another way of touching spiritual reality, something Howard Thurman often wrote about. You discover instances of inspiration and wonder that move beyond and beneath mere cognition.

Maybe your wandering time leads you on a wilderness hike when you cross a ridge and are awestruck by a shimmering alpine lake reflecting a snow-covered mountain peak like a mirror. Or maybe you happen upon a firefly at nightfall in your backyard, where that tiny, sudden light blinks up, rises, and settles on your arm. In simple and unexpected moments of epiphany, you will sense that you are connected to creation in ways that bypass your self-protective, preoccupied, rational mind. Your task? Be attentive. Allow your wonder to wander.

Early in my journey I sought freedom from being absorbed in the world of words that captured much of my life in the politics of Washington, DC. I sought solitary spaces, walks, retreats, and flowing water as an outward journey for this inward quest. Out of the backdoor of my apartment building, I'd walk down and gaze at a holly tree, always green. Reflections turned to how awe-filled encounters with creation can open connection to God.

> AUGUST 16, 1973, AGE 28
> *Nature speaks to us; in sensitive souls it arouses mystic impulses—impulses in which one is moved to moments of awe and inspiration. . . .*
>
> *Whenever one is moved to awe by the beauty of creation, one is moved by God. God, the Creator of both the beauty, and of the inner feelings that excite the soul.*

> *The inspiration we feel in the presence of beauty causes us to transcend ourselves, and in so doing, this is the testimony to the presence of God in the world. Regardless of one's intellectual view of God, when one is moved beyond him or herself, beyond a preoccupation with one's own being to the recognition of the greatness that is other than him or her, then the inward urge to worship and adore such beauty means one is being moved by God toward God. . . .*
>
> *Beauty can prompt us to transcendence; but more than this, it can create another awareness—an awareness that I, as a person, am also part of this creation, that, in fact, I am one with it; that the wonder of creation includes me—but not me as an individuated self; rather, as a part of the whole sweep and force of creation. There can come the awareness that my true self, my "hidden self," is one with all that is beautiful and good; it is one with Christ, who is behind all creation—and in all, over all. And I participate in this realm of existence; the beauty speaks of my true identity, which is not a separated identity at all, but a realization of oneness with God and thus with all—all creation.*

You may find yourself drawn, almost mysteriously, to certain elements of creation, trees, desert landscapes, or water. The imagery is powerful. Teresa of Avila returned to flowing water as her favorite element of creation. Living water, which flows in streams, fountains, springs, rivers, and oceans, connects us to the water of Life. Teresa contrasted this image with water clogged in swamps and puddles, becoming stagnant, just as life gets blocked from the flow of God's presence by our distractions and preoccupations.

In Christian tradition water marks those sacramental moments of passage, transformation, liberation, and rebirth. The children of Israel are set free in the parting of the Red Sea, and then must pass through the Jordan River to enter the promised land. After Jesus's baptism by John, he meets a Samaritan woman by a well, promising her the living water that wells up into life. He then tells Nicodemus that rebirth comes from being born of water and the Spirit. Revelation holds the vision of a healing river flowing from the throne of God for the healing of the nations.

If you feel drawn simply to be near or in water in times of doubt and disillusionment, this may be pointing you to a thirst for the water of life. Your physical connection to water can be sacramental in moments far beyond, and separate from, your baptism. Your body can't live without water, and neither can your soul. Psychology confirms this, as do our dreams and images, where symbols of flowing water, like a river, normally refer to our unconscious life, inviting us into its depths.

As you move from certainty to doubt and even annihilation, bereft of the comfort of secure answers and besieged with deconstructing questions, be attentive to where and when encounters with creation, and its physical elements, provide a fresh connection to God's enduring presence. Dwell there and try to drink deeply. Be open to discover what may begin to well up from within.

Often those experiences find fuller expression in poetry or song than in prosaic description:

<u>June 4, 1993, age 48</u>
Word of the Spirit
Water of life
Oceans of love.
The Spirit hovered over the waters of the deep,
Waters so deep
  So beyond knowing.
Waters surround us, and stretch beyond us;
But our lives are parched, dry bones,
Longing for waters of baptism.
Hanging separated from God, he said, "I thirst."
By the well he offered the woman living waters.
These living waters, filled with grace.
And the Church, is like a boat.
"Oh, the deep, deep love of Jesus,
Vast, unmeasured, boundless, free.
Flowing like a mighty ocean
In its fullness over me."

Sacramental Connections

Once when I was on retreat together with (the now late) Frank Griswold III, Presiding Bishop of the Episcopal Church, we were discussing the nature of Christian unity. Bishop Griswold said: "The Episcopal Church is not held together by some particular creed or Confession. We actually are bonded together by the Book of Common Prayer. It's that shared way of worship that lies at the heart of our identity." Those within tightly woven evangelical systems of theology witnessing a fraying or tearing apart may be drawn to expressions of Christian tradition rooted more in ways of worship than in patterns of belief.

Many of my Catholic friends have lost faith in their tradition's dogmatic systems undergirding its patriarchy and hierarchical authoritarianism. But they are faithfully drawn to the Eucharist, discovering a deep spiritual connection to the mysteries of faith there that otherwise seem hidden by an edifice of doctrinal rigidity. Whether you are Protestant, Catholic, Orthodox, or "None," when your intellectual certitude about faith begins to collapse, you may feel drawn past the structures and systems to sacramental practices and experiences.

A sacrament, broadly speaking, is that physical, tangible vehicle that connects you to the presence of God's Spirit and grace. These aren't merely rites with doctrinal justifications. Rather, understanding them as connectional encounters through common elements like bread, wine, water, and oil that embody mysteriously the reach of God's love into the core of your being may be helpful. Through sacrament, you're invited to receive, and to dwell there.

Integrating the power of sacramental practices and historic liturgy into forms of contemporary worship was something that Robert Webber often spoke of, referring to "ancient-future" faith. His book *Evangelicals on the Canterbury Trail,* first published in 1989, was a prescient forecast of many who would later move on this journey from certainty to connection. He often wrote about this larger movement toward sacramental mystery:

> The story of Christianity moves from a focus on mystery in the classical period, to institution in the medieval era, to individualism in the Reformation era, to reason in the modern era, and, now, in the postmodern era, back to mystery.

Through one path or another, it's likely you may be beckoned toward worship experiences in which you can rest in the mystery of God's presence, connecting you there in ways that are not easily explicable, but nevertheless real. You then are moving through paralyzing doubt into a liberating faith experienced through presence rather than rational proposition. My journey frequently took me there.

MAY 7, 2001, AGE 56
This presence of Christ from the Eucharist this morning dwells in me—in some real way, not just as an idea, and not just as an emotional feeling. Rather, we partake in

this life, and this life dwells in us. That simple truth is overwhelming, almost frightening.

<u>April 9, 2008, age 62</u>
The kind of worship I'm drawn to, beyond question, is a combination of eucharistic liturgy that is rich in feeling and texture. What surprises me is how disinterested I am in "intellectual" pathways to spirituality, in spite of how smart I may be. But I know that to be true.

Living in Sacred Spaces

In this often-bewildering place between certainty and connection, your work in developing a holding space will prove to be essential. It will provide the spiritual infrastructure enabling you to bear uncertainty, which is critical in your transformative process. It will open you to new levels of connection, whether through creation, worship, music, art, or contemplative practices. You might find the distinction that Mircea Eliade, a scholar in comparative religions, made between "sacred space" and "profane space" to be helpful. Eliade examined actual physical places in premodern cultures that were points of shared religious experiences, pointing out how modern societies are uncomfortable with such ideas, regarding most space, in general, as profane, lacking an inherent religious significance, yet we imbue them with meaning and sacredness.

You can apply that as a metaphor for your own lived experience. The default position in modern culture is to live life in a profane space. Your life is caught up in a world saturated by the flow of information and oriented toward emotional and material self-fulfillment. Within that maze, which passes for normalcy, it requires intentionality to carve out sacred space. That's what a variety of spiritual practices, developed habits, and focused attention and intention can do.

Your holding space, in and of itself, doesn't ensure some transformative, spiritual breakthrough. It simply creates the conditions in which a fresh intersection of God's presence in the life may occur. Even though preparing the space with intention, God's presence shows up almost as a divine ambush. In our unknowing, we come to the space with humility, not forcing something to happen, but in a resting detachment to a specific outcome, waiting in that darkness, what mystics such as St. John of the Cross refer to as the dark night of the soul. In this place you embrace a contemplative paradox, yearning for moments of bonding connection, but knowing that emptiness and detachment from all expectation provide spiritual sufficiency. On my own pathway I've found glimmers of God's presence that, small or large, are enough.

January 15, 2009, age 64

As I sat and tried to pray, my mind went in and out, as always. Drifting into some form of sleep, or dreams, but then back. And I realized that what I am trying to do these days, in those moments of mystery, is to touch God, or be touched by God. Beyond ideas, beyond thoughts, it's this yearning to be present to God's life, to God's love. To dwell there, even for a flickering moment. I know this is real. I've been there before, even 37 years ago at Berryville—December, 1972. And I've been back since. Once in a while, but enough.

Trusting in connection rather than clinging to certainty invites you to shed the protective layers of your false self and find comfort in a solitude that welcomes the revelation of your true self. The irony is that the core of your being is not isolated at all but dwells in the deepest connection to God and all that God loves. Meaning all that is. But it is an ongoing journey, continually clearing the debris that clutters your outer and inner life.

Your true self will be discovered in your journey from certainty to connection. And this discovery will liberate you from the ceaseless search for an identity saturated with self-referential exploration, connecting you instead to an incessant, flowing Love that grounds you in Life that absorbs your sense of self into an ocean of wonder, where God's Spirit continues to make all things new. Even in the face of an unfathomable universe, you will embrace these experiences of connection as revealing what is most real.

> *Trusting in connection rather than clinging to certainty invites you to shed the protective layers of your false self.*

Making all things new is the process of transformation. But that never is limited to your own personal life. The previous boundary between a private existence and your connection with others and the whole world will be severed in the discovery of your true self. This transformation fuses you with others in the ongoing movement of God's love in the world. Your connection is to a future, breaking into the pain and injustice of the present, with power, promise and hope. And you are sustained partaking mysteriously in this Life.

VI.

From Grandiosity to Authenticity

Richard Rohr was already seated in a booth at the High Noon Restaurant and Saloon in Old Town Albuquerque when Kaarin and I arrived to meet him for dinner. We had known each other from earlier years when we were part of the Sojourners community and Richard was a teacher and leader at the New Jerusalem Community in Cincinnati.

In the intervening years Richard moved to Albuquerque and started the Center for Action and Contemplation. When we met in Albuquerque, Kaarin and I were thinking about beginning a new chapter of our lives, reaching the close of our vocation careers under the sunny skies of New Mexico.

Earlier that week Kaarin and I had decided to take an online Enneagram test. We had been curious about the Enneagram and knew friends who were devotees. Previously we had become well acquainted with the Myers-Briggs Personality Inventory, and I had used it in various working environments. But the Enneagram was fresh and different. We watched as the Enneagram became widely used in approaches to spiritual formation and psychological insight within the Christian community and beyond.

Reading this book, you are probably a faith leader, social activist, pastor, priest, or committed lay person desiring to work for God's justice in the world. A major challenge you face is the public image or persona others project onto you as a model for faith in action. You can become attached to that in a way that disregards your personal authenticity. Unattended, this can unravel your life. The Enneagram, I've found, is a tool that can guard you against that danger because it brings insight into the strengths and vulnerabilities of your basic personality.

Engaging the Enneagram

In the 1970s Richard Rohr was introduced to the Enneagram by his spiritual director. And before it became widely known, he started using it within the New Jerusalem Community. By 1990, with Andreas Ebert, he published *Discovering the Enneagram: An Ancient Tool for a New Spiritual Journey*. A decade later, as interest grew, they wrote another book, *The Enneagram: A Christian Perspective*. It became a runaway best seller. In this work Rohr and Ebert uncovered how the Enneagram's roots could be found within the early writings of the desert fathers, and then showing up centuries later in forms of Sufi mysticism before being rediscovered more recently as a tool compatible and popularized within Christian spiritual formation.

So when Kaarin and I met with Richard Rohr for a memorable dinner of New Mexican food, we feasted the whole evening on the Enneagram, its roots, its uses, and its applications. More than just another classification of personality characteristics, Richard stressed, the Enneagram can best be understood as a mirror into one's soul. It uncovers the roots of those external traits, preoccupations, habits, and fixations that form one's false self, like the layers of clay providing the outward, protective shell for the Buddha in Thailand. As Rohr and Ebert write: The Enneagram is "a very ancient Christian tool for the discernment of spirits, the struggle with our capital sin, our 'false self,' and the encounter with our True Self in God."

At its most basic, the Enneagram posits that people fall into one of nine basic "types" that rest at the interior foundations of personality and form a matrix for the stance and disposition shaping their life in the world. These types, however, are not static; rather, they form the context for development either in healthy, integrated ways, or in unhealthy, dysfunctional directions. Often the structure of the Enneagram is visually depicted as a circle with nine points or types, which are in various interactive relationships with one another, and are classified in groups of three, centered either in the "gut," the "heart," or the "head."

I told Richard that the online Enneagram test revealed that I was a Type Three. Often this is called the Achiever. There's a strong motivation to succeed, to display competency and skill in the tasks the Achiever takes on. And Threes are also emotionally dependent on competency, living off praise from others. They exhibit persuasive, attractive qualities and are intuitively attuned to ways others react to them as they cultivate the approval that inwardly they so desperately desire.

At one level, the drive to achieve and succeed is laudable. Many influential leaders are Enneagram Threes, including Bill Wilson (the founder of AA) and Mitt Romney, as well as, Ebert notes, Dorothy Day.

An Enneagram type is never an indictment but merely a description of your basic inward psychological wiring. What matters is how you understand, accept, and work with these qualities, which can lead either to integration and health—what some call a "redeemed" Enneagram type—or toward disintegration and unhealth.

Because of their drive to succeed and need for praise, Threes can become image conscious, determined to share the best commercial of themselves. And this is how Threes like me can get into trouble, because we begin to shade the truth, telling the best parts of the marvelous stories about ourselves and leaving off the other realities. As this subtle self-glorification grows, deceit sets in as Threes become increasingly detached and blind to who they really are. Becoming alienated from their own inner feelings, they lose their capacity for empathy toward others.

Healthy or "redeemed" Enneagram Threes learn to face their inner life and become self-accepting, usually through experiences that are detached and secluded from public praise. On this pathway Threes can move toward authenticity, and become models capable of inspiring others toward shared goals.

"As children Threes were often loved not for their own sake," Richard writes in *The Enneagram*, "but were praised and rewarded when they were successful and had special achievements to show for it." Over dinner we talked about how this can get played out. In your story of seeking affirmation through achievement and success, vanity might become endemic. And the inflationary pressures on the ego combined with your need to convey an attractive, compelling public image can result in grandiosity.

For those who recognize these pressures to present a compelling image, whether you are a Three or not, the Enneagram is helpful, as it can function as spiritual and psychological "truth serum." It provides an inner template of the dynamics beneath your outward proclivities and patterns and then invites you into an honest and often painful engagement as the pathway to a healthy integrated life. For me, that dinner conversation in New Mexico helped me to see not only where I was on the Enneagram chart, but also the work I was being called to do to move toward wholeness.

Pride Evolving into Grandiosity

Grandiosity is pride on steroids. And, of course, it's not limited to a specific Enneagram type. In contemporary culture grandiosity has become an almost necessary ingredient of social and professional success. Social media have created the ubiquitous new marketplace for self-promotion. We curate the best image of ourselves through content we post, through clever words, through presenting exceptional experiences, and through the number of friends and followers we attract. While there are various apps that also provide valuable relational connections with others, our default habits on social media push us to project an edited version of ourselves we hope will appeal to or impress others. It's far easier in this snappy, click-happy digital world to be grandiose than to be authentic.

Each of the starting points in the four movements of the soul—self-sufficiency, certainty, grandiosity, and control—are not simply wrong or bad in a binary way. All can meet some real need and carry a measure of helpful truth. That's certainly the case with pride, the precursor of grandiosity. But even so, each of these is a starting point that begins a journey which can free you from clinging to a false, external self and lead you into deeper authenticity.

In my hometown of Santa Fe, I've joined in the Pride Parade with church groups as locals gathered from a wide range of communities to form one supportive community for LGBTQ persons—from the sanitarian drivers with their trucks to rangers from the National Park Service accompanied by Buddy Bison and Smokey the Bear. What's clear is that any group that has been marginalized, repressed, and persecuted simply for who they are yearns for and deserves a public response that conveys pride in their identity.

There is a distinction between pride in your inner core identity, affirming the inherent dignity of every person, bearing the image of God, and that prideful attachment to your external successes and achievements. Grandiosity seeps in, sometimes in hidden ways, when your inner self holds insecurity and doubts about your inherent self-worth, prompting an addictive dependence on the praise of others. If and when, for whatever wounded reasons, you have buried deeply rooted feelings of your inner worthlessness, the praise of others will become a perpetual narcotic that is never enough.

For those on the justice journey, whether activists, theological students, pastors, or Catholic sisters in a community hosting a retreat center—whatever your vocational calling—you're a person committed to making a difference in the world. Regardless of your Enneagram type, you're geared toward achievement and working toward goals, even when this is sought through service to unhoused persons in an interfaith shelter, or ministry in a parish of aging members with a future jeopardized by dwindling demographics. You want to help, to succeed, and that desire is virtually inbred in our individualistic, competitive culture.

Your challenge, at whatever stage in your journey, is to be alert to the ways in which pride lives in you and to prevent it from morphing into grandiosity. This doesn't come by beating up your ego with doctrines about your total depravity. Rather, it requires a spiritual and psychological detachment from rooting your identity and sense of self-worth in what you are achieving. Absorbing the interior wisdom that prevents you from defining yourself by your accomplishments is your work to do. Or in theological parlance, attending to the persistent temptation of "works righteousness."

Grandiosity, like all these starting points for the four movements of the soul, is the point for beginning an arduous task that must be nurtured by your habitual attention to your inward journey in the midst of your outward callings. Normally, it seems to take a lifetime for this movement. But you'll know when you're on the path leading, step by step, toward an integrated life. This will come as you begin to sense who you really are, before God, and discover moments when your soul feels at rest.

Lack of attention to the corrosive growth of grandiosity can become treacherous. Chuck DeGroat, on the faculty of Western Theological Seminary in Holland, Michigan, has written about the dangers in *When Narcissism Comes to Church: Healing your Community from Emotional and Spiritual Abuse.* He describes the devastating, infectious effects of narcissism related to each of the Enneagram types and portrays how pastors and spiritual leaders unleash abuse, violating the trust of their communities, due to failure in giving essential attention to their own inner wounds and needs. His description of one whose grandiosity is infused with narcissism is haunting:

> This face of narcissism often looks like the classic caricature of *grandiose* narcissism—the charming, superior, exceptional person. They have an almost desperate need to be seen. The thrill of accomplishment is like a dopamine-high, leading to an addictive need for more. Workaholism is a common feature, but often they ascend to positions of leadership, demanding the same drivenness from others. Out of touch with their inner feelings and needs, they remain at the emotional surface, often

incapable of empathy or real connection. Yet they feed off applause and affection. They live for the win. Perhaps more importantly, they are terrified of failure.

Noticing the Signs, Listening to Dreams

Decades before I had ever heard of the Enneagram, I had glimmerings of grandiosity. As a young novice in my tentative inward journey amid the allure of political life on Capitol Hill, I identified unflattering realities:

> JANUARY 11, 1970, AGE 24
> *It was clear that to deny self—for me—meant the denial of pretension, of vain-glory, of dreams of grandeur, of status and reputation, of idolization—all these things. Who I am, how I look, how I dress, what I say, etc.—I must give it all up—it must not be my idol, my god. I must strive only to serve and love.*

But simply intellectually identifying a danger isn't dealing with it emotionally and spiritually. Four years later I was still treading the same psychological water:

> DECEMBER 15, 1973, AGE 28
> *What does it mean for me to be emptied? . . . What hit me with real force was how I still thought I was "somebody." How I thought I was more important than other people. . . .*

> *So if I am to be emptied, I must be emptied of that kind of pride. The pride that likes to think of myself as more important than others—as meriting special consideration, deserving a special place. It is this subtle pride that must be forgiven, and emptied if Christ is to be born within me.*

It takes your holding space, which nurtures regular practices, to move through these soulful transitions. And the movement from grandiosity to authenticity, like other transitions, is never linear. It's cyclical, cycling back through familiar psychological territory but developing a deeper spiritual capacity to accept, to trust, and to relinquish. So the pattern is like a repetitive spiral that, as it circles back, breaks through again and moves forward.

Recognition of the starting point for each movement, in this case grandiosity, begins by encountering the power of the obstacles you face. And these will reemerge at the points of your life's critical transitions, like a marriage, a vocational choice, a new calling, an ordination, a change in jobs, a physical move, a divorce, or death of a loved one. At any point when normal frameworks of exterior security are altered or disrupted, you are likely to feel, even unconsciously, a pull back toward the behaviors and impulses that have fortified your false self.

Sometimes, especially if you're not attuned to your underlying emotional and spiritual tensions, your dreams may put you on notice. Deciphering them may take the assistance of a skilled therapist, spiritual director, or friend. But that's inner work well worth doing. And the biblical precedents of prophets, kings, priests, disciples, and apostles, as well as Mary and Joseph, whose journeys are radically revealed and altered through dreams, are manifold. Most modern, intellectualized versions of Western Christianity tend to overlook and dismiss these testimonies, but prophetic voices like Martin Luther King, Jr., noted dreams and shared them, as with his famous speech, whose words as he described to Mahalia Jackson, came to him in a kind of high-intensity dream.

Dreams may speak to us, teach us, awaken us to truths, and form a prophetic call. In my life there have been many instances of this, but one especially comes to mind. In 1988, Kaarin and I were trying to make one of our most difficult decisions about the direction and calling of our lives. We had to move from Missoula, Montana, with our two young children. The move would take us either to a position in Michigan or to an as-yet-uncertain possibility of a position with the World Council of Churches in Geneva, Switzerland. My dreams revealed my inner turmoil:

FEBRUARY 18, 1988, AGE 42

A dream. I am somewhere like an Army or Air Force chapel. It burns, is under attack, and is destroyed. I am to be the chaplain—the one in charge. Someone speaks, whom I overhear, about how I would be ideal to build a new chapel even on another site.

> *Then, we all are gathered around tables. I am the one in charge of the chapel and program, waiting to be introduced. . . . I've rearranged the tablecloths to make them even and I'm busy.*

A short while later the position at a seminary in Michigan collapsed. I was defensive and angry. My therapist pointed to the grandiosity involved on my part. In fact, my dream of February 18, she said, was, "very grand." I wanted to cling strongly to what I felt I deserved to do and what others expected.

A turbulent time of insecurity continued, even after I received word from the general secretary of the World Council of Churches that I had been selected to be the new director of Church and Society. A difficult process of mutual relinquishment eventually brought our family to Geneva.

An initial task assigned to me was to develop a WCC position paper on the ethics of biotechnology and to bring this process to the meeting of its governing body, the Central Committee, in Moscow. There I had another dream:

JANUARY 16, 1990, AGE 44
> *I recalled a dream—I was in some kind of prison, or interrogation, and as a punishment, I was being prodded, like pushed or pressured from behind, to keep going, to keep running ahead. And then it stopped. I wondered if the dream was about my pressuring myself to succeed, to achieve, to do well—the gifted child syndrome.*

At one level or another pride stalks most of our psyches, seeking to puff up our self-worth by clinging to ephemeral experiences of success that bypass where our deepest self is rooted. It's a lifelong spiritual calling, I believe, to become deeply detached from a psychological dependence on how others react to us.

Dr. David Wang, a professor of psychology at Fuller Theological Seminary, received funding from the Templeton Foundation to coordinate a global study on how seminary education affects the spiritual development of students. An early empirical piece of data revealed that 45 percent of seminary students are engaged in "impression management." They spend emotional energy trying to shape and mold the kind of impression they make on others. Left undiscovered or denied, it's easy to imagine how such a student becomes a pastor or priest habituated to a grandiosity that shapes an external image alienated from his or her true self. Beware. For that's the soil from which the abuse of power grows.

Grandiosity before a Fall

Taking a close look at admired and successful public figures we can sometimes spot the malignant growth of grandiosity. In my work as the general secretary of the Reformed Church in America, I had gotten to know the late Bob Schuller, known for leading the highly popular Hour of Power TV broadcast and building the Crystal Cathedral. Part of our denomination, Dr. Schuller's influence was enormous, and global. Countless times in ecumenical travel around the world I'd hear from people thankful for the ways the Hour of Power had blessed and encouraged them in ministry.

When I first went to visit Bob in his California office, he showed me the framed baptismal gown hanging on the wall that he had worn as an infant when baptized at a small RCA church in Iowa. He has called that gown his most prized possession. But as he showed me the gown, tears welled up in his eyes. He admitted that he had never felt fully affirmed and accepted by his denominational family, and he was wounded by that deficit despite his worldwide fame and success. Something he clearly craved. I wondered why such a gifted person, who had achieved such enormous success, would still seek approval.

Over time it seemed to me that in his powerful, inspiring sermons about possibility thinking, he was often preaching to himself.

Dr. Schuller's stellar career ended tragically. Like many highly effective leaders whose inward, unexamined fragile egos are protected by grandiosity, giving up power can feel mortally threatening. This is often seen with founding pastors of new congregations, inspiring leaders of social movements, countless politicians (including some recent presidents), activists who have successfully built vital organizations, megachurch pastors who have spawned multiplying worship centers, and many others. What I saw in Bob, I also saw in myself. Perhaps that's why I was so attuned to it. Maybe you can see this in yourself, too.

In Bob Schuller's case, he was never able to transfer power, even to his own son. In a complex story of familial and organizational dysfunction, a fifty-million-dollar ministry went bankrupt, and the Crystal Cathedral was sold to the Catholic Archdiocese of Orange to pay debts.

Success and achievement don't diminish grandiosity. They inflate it. Our movement toward authenticity has to begin inwardly, away from the crowds. It requires detachment from the fruit of our actions. And that's one definition of prayer.

Success and achievement don't diminish grandiosity. They inflate it. Our movement toward authenticity has to begin inwardly, away from the crowds.

It's important to also be alert to how grandiosity can breed contempt and destroy solidarity. At the public, political level that is devastatingly obvious. Grandiose nationalism breeds contempt for the "other," making them victims, destroying social solidarity and perpetuating lies about the nation's true identity. But personally, the same dynamics are in play. Your grandiosity and mine, as you read in those journal excerpts, create a subtle superiority toward others, fueling pretension, sanctioning a judgmental disposition, and shrinking capacity for social empathy and real, rather than rhetorical, compassion.

Strength through Weakness?

Authenticity requires a movement through the encounter of desolation rather than the celebration of success. Two thousand years ago the apostle Paul, himself a tortured but highly gifted leader, gave startling, self-disclosing advice about dealing with grandiosity and authenticity in his second recorded letter to the young, struggling church at Corinth. "I will not boast, except of my weaknesses. . . . I refrain from it, so that no one may think better of me than what is seen in me or heard from me, even considering the exceptional character of the revelations." He continues in this passage to share about the "thorn in his flesh," which he sees as given to him to prevent him from becoming too elated, despite his pleas for the thorn to be removed. Paul concludes his reflection by sharing the word from God that he received in response to his pleas: "My grace is sufficient for you, for power is made perfect in weakness" (2 Cor 12:5–7, 9).

Biblical scholars disagree about what Paul's "thorn in the flesh" actually was. That's hardly the point. Those in the Corinthian congregation knew exactly what he meant. Paul was sharing here his transparent struggle to not cling to the outward attributes of his false self and inflate his reputation by boasting about his revelations. Strength coming through weakness was as countercultural then as it is now. And rooting one's identity in the sufficiency of God's grace was as hard for Paul, who had to subvert a whole religious and cultural system of "works righteousness," as it is for you and me. But this is what precisely opens the door to the pathway toward authenticity.

Any activist, pastor, or leader will have a hard time believing that "strength is made perfect in weakness." But this isn't about denying your abilities, gifts, talents, or brilliance. Rather, it's all about where you root your inner security, and what you trust to be at the core of your identity. Are you riveted, far more than you realize, to the outward reflection of your image? Is that where you try to find strength? If so, it's a recipe for living an inauthentic life.

Any number of crises may push you to realize that the strengths you've become dependent upon are not invincible as the external scaffolding of your ego collapses. For me, this occurred once around a vocational crisis. In the rarified ecumenical life of the World Council of Churches, my work as director of Church and Society thrived in a trajectory bolstered by widespread acclamation. Then, an internal reorganization established four units to carry all the WCC's work, including one on justice, peace, and creation. It required a director, and staff colleagues encouraged me to apply. It felt like the next predictable step forward.

However, the new WCC general secretary reached out privately to a former staff colleague then back in Kenya, inviting him to apply and appointing him to the position. I was devastated. What startled me was the depth of my anger and emotional desolation. In my journal I tried to process the pain:

> MAY 25, 1993, AGE 48
> *All my life I've been rewarded for being the "good person." Everything I've wanted I've generally achieved. Each position has come about, with recognition, etc. Now, at the WCC, I have been the "good person." I've done everything right, produced good work, received recognition. Except*

> *that now, I've not been rewarded as a result. Instead, I am marginalized institutionally.*
>
> *So how do I respond?*
>
> *Why have I been the "good person"—to achieve reward? Am I caught in the same cycle from my youth?*
>
> *One question returns. How do I get nurture? Through my accomplishments? I have been deeply upset and depressed since not being appointed as Unit III director. . . . I feel such anger at being marginalized, and I must discover the roots of this anger. . . .*
>
> *I realize now these things: First, I have not been functioning out of a spiritual center in my work at the WCC in recent time. I feel spiritually disoriented.*
>
> *Second, too much of my ego and identity was tied up in the position of director, and my "position" in the Council.*

In the crucible of dross being consumed, you will surely face your own version of a time like this, whether coming from a vocational failure, a personal crisis, an emotional breakdown, a spiritual disillusionment, or maybe all of these. Your pride and grandiosity will be revealed as no more than clanging cymbals deflecting attention from the sounds of your soul.

You'll have the chance, however, to shatter the reflected image of your false self and glimpse who you truly are and are called to become. You have the opportunity—the invitation—to pay attention. Remember that even your dreams may speak, interpret, and point the way, as mine did:

JANUARY 25, 1995, AGE 49
A dream. There's a kid, and he smashes his face against the glass mirror, to break it. . . . Is this part of me, smashing a reflection of myself in a mirror to free myself?

It's freedom that the deepest part of yourself yearns for. Not a freedom that centers on narcissistic notions of self, inflating your ego. Rather, it's liberation from the obsessive, self-absorbed reactivity borne from being bound to the responses of others as the barometer of your well-being. And it's liberation from reliance on the protectionist, perfectionist self-image you compulsively curate. In my experience, that true freedom comes only when you grasp that you dwell in, are held by, and are absorbed by, God's love.

As the Beloved

The late Henri Nouwen had the gift of putting recognizable experiences of our spiritual and psychological journeys into illumining words and truths. In *The Return of the Prodigal Son*, a brilliant reflection on Rembrandt's painting of that parable, Nouwen uncovers the penetrating power of hearing God's voice assuring you that you are truly beloved, just like the prodigal son, who was embraced by his father. And Nouwen describes what internalizing that truth means in words I think are particularly profound for those involved in ministry, activism, leadership, and service:

> As the Beloved, I can confront, console, admonish and encourage without fear of rejection or need of affirmation. As the Beloved, I can suffer persecution without desire for revenge and receive praise without using it as a proof of my goodness.

Those are words I've held close, printed and made like a home page. For anyone seeking authenticity I recommend you put those words in a place that can regularly attract your attention. They will be there for your faltering movements from grandiosity to authenticity. And put you back on the path.

When you're in the presence of someone living as the Beloved, who models authenticity, someone living out of his or her true self, here's how you know it. You become excited about God's purpose for yourself. You become inspired to live more fully into your calling. You find deeper energy and promise in your community, your organization, or your movement. Around those who know themselves, who have internalized being the Beloved, the focus is no longer around them. Rather, they have become a vehicle, a channel, for an outpoured love that now is touching you. There's no mistaking it.

The person who powerfully conveyed to me what it was like to live out of being God's Beloved was my spiritual director, Gordan Cosby. When I first began trying to embed a new inward journey in my outward, activist, crusading life in Washington's politics, he exuded a sense of the Beloved. He lived into it. Many years later, shortly before his death, when my life had carried me to unexpected destinations, I met with him at the Potter's House. As we sat down, his immediate question was, "Wes, how is it with your inner spirit?" I thought, *That's it: It's really the only question to ask.* It's the question that grows the sense of belovedness in others. I hope in your journey you find someone who will ask you that question.

On your journey you'll find that authenticity comes in sporadic flashes. You may get an early taste of a life relinquished to the presence of God's merciful love, loosening the grip of your pride and grandiosity. But it won't last, even after a dramatic Damascus Road conversion experience. That's why you will find it imperative to construct a holding space to continually internalize momentary invasions of grace and confront the pain that will also mark your journey.

Often overlooked after Saul's life-changing encounter, becoming Paul, is that he retreated to Arabia for about three years before going to Jerusalem. I wonder if he was constructing his own holding space after the deconstruction of his prior, grandiose pattern of belief and self-righteous action. The holding space you can construct will open your inner life so that breakthroughs of liberating grace can begin to become more predictable, rather than tantalizing but illusive.

Shedding grandiosity and pride in a quest for authenticity can feel like peeling away the layers of an onion. Cultivating habitual practices of interior attention, however, can build your capacity to focus on the real questions that touch your soul, and subvert the distracting, false attempts to silence them.

In September 2022, I was flying to Germany to be an adviser at the World Council of Churches 11th Assembly in Karlsruhe, with its theme, "Christ's Love Moves the World to Reconciliation and Unity." Years earlier, in 2003, I had been among those nominated to be general secretary of the WCC. I was one of the final candidates. But after an arduous process of discernment, I could not hear deep within a clear calling or a peace with my true self, so I withdrew. In my journal, almost two decades later, I was pondering my presence at the WCC Assembly, and where my journey, with its persistent inner inquiries, had taken me:

> AUGUST 30, 2022, AGE 77
> *Reflecting on this discovery and comfort with my true self. Not the false self, absorbed with my ego, with the stories about me, or what still could be. Those are fantasies infused with my prelacy. They can be sent aside. Instead, the focus on what is real, on who I am, on who I am called to be, and how I am to live in this finishing chapter of my life.*

Living Authentically, Hearing a Call

What does authenticity really mean? What, for you, would an authentic life look like? Your journey, of course, is distinctive, emanating from your own peculiar and precious internal wiring and external calling. But a durable holding space will nurture a movement common to any of our journeys. In one of his July 2024 meditations from the Center for Action and Contemplation, Richard Rohr describes it this way:

> The sustained practice of contemplation involves letting go of all the things that we use to define our so-called separate selves. It helps us access our True Self, the part of us that is always connected to God. Contemplation teaches us how to live in this open space.

There's a mystery in how the movement into the presence of God at the deepest level of your being leads to the uncovering of your true self. This annihilates so many of the securities that have bolstered your ego's formation of your identity. But I believe you will discover that is the curious pathway toward authenticity.

Often this becomes linked to an outward calling. The process of hearing God's call is in reality a quest to embrace your true identity. It's not doing the right thing. It's about being the right person, the one who hears that he or she is beloved and is called forth from that grounding, empowering experience.

That will lead you to an outward journey of activism, ministry, or vocational service. Maybe that means you'll be a part in starting a transformational social movement, or heralding a prophetic message, or forming a new community, or becoming a political player, or leading a nonprofit advocacy or service group, or serving the life of the organized church. But you will be propelled not by a cause but by a call. You will be living out of a genuine, humbling, even annihilating encounter with the Living God.

You see this throughout the narrative stories in the Bible, especially the prophets. Consider Isaiah's formative experience in the presence of the Holy One in the sixth chapter, which then sends him on his mission. Or Moses with the burning bush. Or my favorite, Jonah. He wants to evade this encounter but is swallowed up by desolation and darkness. It took more than just a crack for the light to get into Jonah's being. But this bewildering, transforming experience results in the grounding of God's calling. You'll find, in one way or another, that this is the pattern. Discovering your authentic self, rooted in God's presence at the core of your being, will disrupt your journey. It will confound your calculated expectations. It will interrupt your normalcy. And from it, you will come to know a calling.

But you will be propelled not by a cause, but by a call.

This is a countercultural way of moving through your vocational paths. It's normal to seek appealing positions in organizations, academic institutions, the church, and social movements. And you may not have reflected on the deeper, inner reasons for why those positions seem appealing. In subtle ways you've probably learned how to present yourself in ways that get you promoted. That's true whether you are serving within the church or with Amnesty International. But living your life on basis of call is a radically different point of departure.

Early in my journey, at Church of the Saviour's Dayspring Farm retreat center, I heard Dorothy Devers, the retreat leader, share about the dangers of "prelacy." It's a word I had never heard. An old-fashioned term, *prelacy* usually refers to church leaders, like bishops in high positions of authority, sometimes as a group, and underscores the dignity due to them. But Dorothy linguistically repurposed this as the pride of place and position. One builds his or her esteem, and expects it from others, from the external position one holds. As prelacy deepens its grip on your ego, it strengthens your drive to preserve your position, becoming defensive about your actions, and perhaps prompting you to seek another post of even greater positional authority. In this understanding, prelacy is the handmaiden of grandiosity and the enemy of authenticity.

As seen in biblical examples and echoed in the lives of many inspiring persons through history—those whom some church traditions call saints—the gateway into authenticity, bringing the discovery of your true self, leads through pain and loss. You don't have to rely on spiritual or theological explanations to understand this. It emerges at times in culture, where novels, movies, and songs testify to this wisdom.

Hearing Wisdom from Other Voices

In June 2024, author Joyce Maynard published *How the Light Gets In*, a sequel to her best-selling 2021 novel, *Count the Ways*. The story centers on the dynamics of a family, disrupted by tragedy, dysfunction, and loss. The husband is deceased and

Eleanor is a matriarch navigating through the turbulent years of 2010 to 2024. When the novel was released, Maynard was interviewed by Scott Simon on NPR's *Weekend Edition*. Here's part of that exchange:

> *Simon:* And as you say, the lessons aren't in our triumphs. They're in our failures.
> *Maynard:* That's what the title is about. That's what Leonard Cohen meant. I will say of my own life—and I think most people at this stage of life would say the same—that things didn't turn out the way we imagined. . . . Life brings you to your knees. . . . And the lessons that I value most, probably in just about every case, have come from my failures, my losses.

It's one thing to recognize this truth in the latter chapters of your life. But it's so much more valuable to grasp this wisdom early in your journey. You'll be able to deter having your pain catapult your life into desperate and destructive actions of denial and addictive gratification. And you'll be less likely to cling to power and control by blaming others for your failures and by shirking ownership of your inner wounds.

Consider another example from culture that illumines a spiritual reality. Cory Richards, a well-known photographer for *National Geographic*, was recognized for his high-energy mountaineering exploits, and, while they yielded spectacular pictures, they also frequently threatened his life. You could say he sought positional authority in a literal geographical way, determined to conquer the world's highest peaks. In 2011, he survived an avalanche in the Himalayas and recorded it on video. Then, in 2016, he ascended to the summit of Mt. Everest without using oxygen, one of only two-hundred people to do so, and documented the event on Snapchat.

But the attention and fame from these outward, upward journeys covered an unattended internal life riddled with mental instability, chaos, betrayal, and addiction. In 2024, he shared the reality of his life in a self-disclosing memoir, *The Color of Everything: A Journey to Quiet the Chaos Within*. In an interview with NPR's Sacha Pfeiffer, she introduces Richards as "a stereotype of this dashing, itinerant adventure photographer and the wild life that comes with it." At one point she posed this query:

> *Sacha Pfeiffer:* You also note that survival sells stories. And as you survived and were able to sell stories, you sold more photos. So it kind of propelled you forward because it had a positive effect on your career.
>
> *Richards:* One of the things that I started to realize is that a very successful career does not always a healthy brain make. I look at somebody's success and I go, "They must be really happy and really healthy," when in fact there was proof in my own life that that isn't true and unraveling that was

really hard. Because when I let go of those identities, I really question what place I have in the world and what is my value here. And how do I find it if I'm not those things?

Liberating Your True Self

Encountering the reality of your pain and loss, and confronting the inability of your success to satisfy your soul's desires, can breed a detachment from your false self. It will undermine your attempts to ground your inner security in a superficial, exterior identity. And detachment will be essential for your authenticity to emerge. That's how you'll answer the questions identified by Cory Richards, and all those on this journey from grandiosity to authenticity as false identities are shed: What place do I have in the world? What is my value? How do I find it if not in those things?

In your spiritual life, answering these question will also alter your understanding of your "gifts." The tendency in various forms of spirituality is to regard your gifts as your possessions. And a variety of books, tools, and techniques are on offer to yield the discovery of your gifts. This focus makes an important contribution particularly in attempts to empower the laity within Christian traditions that concentrate authority on priests and pastors through their ordained ministry. But it also can inhibit the movement to a deep authenticity.

When you find moments that liberate your true self, like the gold emerging from the refiner's fire that reflects back the image of God, all your life is experienced as gift. And the particular "gifts," capacities, contributions, and abilities you exercise are not really your own, because you have tasted life beyond the illusion of the isolated, separate self. Your advocacy, your preaching, your writing, your teaching, your service, your witness—all of these draw on your natural capacities and gifts, but they are detached from your ego. They are not your possessions. Rather, they are given to you to exercise with abandon, and they are then given away, because that's the nature of the love—God's love—which has claimed your soul.

VII.

From Control to Trust

David Whyte, Irish poet, consultant, and writer, has brought his poetic wisdom to writing about organizational leadership related to his consulting work with major corporations. His book, *The Heart Aroused: Poetry and Preservation of the Soul of Corporate America,* found many readers attracted to this integrated vision.

"It only takes one line of poetry to change your life," Whyte writes. And his poem, "What to Remember upon Waking," contains such a line, the kind of line that can launch you on the journey from *control* to *trust:* "What you can plan is too small for you to live."

We seem addicted to planning, born out of a compulsion to control. I'm sure you've experienced this—if not the addiction, then the sense that you need to be in control. And if you are involved in the governance of any organization, institution, company, congregation, or nonprofit agency, you've gone through a strategic planning process, and maybe several. I've been through more than I can remember, at times leading them. But I've lost faith in five-year plans. When speaking to groups recently, I've begun saying that I'm not initiating any more strategic planning exercises. And the response, each time, is laughter followed by applause.

Something is happening within the life of organizations in our society as we meet the limitations of standard approaches to effective governance and performance. We don't have the capacity to predict the future and control events in ways the culture taught us was an assumed quantity. A small light is leaking through the cracks, though. In some circles healthy humility and curiosity have begun to emerge regarding the limits of control, planning, and what's clearly an unknown future.

Three Unexpected Disruptions

Any of the institutions, movements, and groups you serve and work with have experienced major, unexpected disruptions in the past few years. The first was the COVID pandemic. This was never foreseen, despite general concerns about global pandemics and better procedures. But no external event in the last decade has had a more pervasive and disorienting impact on society's common life. Within weeks, so many plans and goals no longer made sense. And our daily interactions within society were radically altered.

The life of each religious congregation—and there are about 350,000 local churches and houses of worship in the United States—was seriously disrupted. You may participate in one of them, and perhaps are a pastor, priest, teacher, or other leader in one of them. Beyond all expectation or control, the COVID pandemic changed them all: How to worship, do education, perform sacraments, minister to those who are ill, serve the marginalized, engage in mission, and even how to define membership. Studies are showing that COVID mostly accelerated trends already present in congregational life, with both negative and positive consequences. But every congregation had to decide how to respond to this unanticipated disruption. Any of its strategic plans, if in place, were rendered largely irrelevant.

The same held true, of course, throughout other social organizations and groups in society. What is striking is how so much of our institutional life and social behaviors were decisively affected by external events that could not have been predicted or controlled. No one's strategic plan included this.

Another significant event of the last decade was George Floyd's murder by police, erupting into the racial reckoning around not only the country, but the globe. Recall how your own journey was affected by Derek Chauvin's knee on the neck of a Black man in Minneapolis on May 25, 2020, and its aftermath. The response that ensued was never predicted nor foreseen. Like a spark igniting long-accumulated tinder into a conflagration, Floyd's murder evoked a massive reckoning that confronted institutions, organizations, companies, churches, political parties, foundations, and the media with the depth of ingrained racial injustice and the imperative of radical change. Its reverberations, as well as a resulting political and social backlash, have continued to ripple through society to today.

These sudden events overwhelmed the planning—including so-called contingency planning—and capacities for control by educational establishments, governmental agencies, and social institutions. Agendas were radically altered. In many cases the urgency of addressing the cancerous, continuous legacy of racial injustice dramatically changed commitments, priorities and actions of countless organizations to extents never envisioned by any of their strategic planning.

Climate catastrophes have also disrupted planning and revealed the pretentious predictions of control by local governments, federal agencies, and relief organizations. Scorching, record-breaking heat, unprecedented wildfires, and historically catastrophic hurricanes and floods have obliterated prevailing predictions and explanations of "normal ranges." In my home state of New Mexico a wildfire in 2023 was the worst in the state's history, meeting a state vastly unprepared. Similar stories with apocalyptic images come from Los Angeles, Oregon, Maui, the Texas coast, and the path of hurricanes sweeping up the Eastern seaboard.

These events beyond human control intervene in social life in ways that devastate normalcy. They strike beyond the margins of our planning. Their impact demonstrates the futility of trusting in the efficacy of our institutions to protect us against extreme climate catastrophes that will continue to escalate.

These three disruptions, and more that you may have had directly affect your life and work, highlight the imperative of building organizational resilience rather than perfecting strategic planning. Nurturing the capacity to recognize new realities, rapidly adapt actions, and discover creative responses, rather than clinging to earlier hopes of control, chart the pathway toward the radical revitalization of social institutions. If you have any level of leadership responsibility, put that five-year plan on the shelf and refocus your energy on change and adaptation.

The Illusion of Control

However, your far more fundamental and formidable challenge is closer to home: to relinquish the obsessive belief in control that pervades your personal journey. This parallels the dynamics of organizations, where clinging to a desire to control outcomes through painstaking strategic planning gets emasculated by major, unexpected disruptions. It also confronts the personal placement of your trust, asking you to let go of assumptions and habits you've learned to propel your way forward in life. This challenge strikes at the heart of your spiritual understanding and practice. What do you do when you are asked to—forced to—step away from your indefatigable belief in your ability to plan and control your life's outcomes?

To embark on this journey from control to trust, realize that others have paved the way. Step One of the twelve steps of the Alcoholics Anonymous process starts us on the path. This is not about whether you suffer from the imprisonment of addiction to alcohol or substances. However, if you personally have participated in AA, or are close to a family member or friend who has, you'll be a step ahead.

The entry point into the twelve steps of AA is an admission of your powerlessness—specifically, powerlessness over alcohol. But more generally, it involves confronting the illusions of your ability to be in control. As AA explains, Step One is the opposite of encouraging self-confidence. Contrary to the popular self-improvement myths in our culture, it doesn't begin by instilling faith in your mastery. Rather, it takes root in utter humility. This echoes what you discovered in the movement from grandiosity to authenticity, namely, that strength is made perfect in weakness.

There's a deep, countercultural irony involved here. It requires unmasking the faith rooted in our own ego to overcome the threats and obstacles that life will inevitably present. Instead, an internal, spiritual surrender is the starting point. Rabbi Rami Shapiro describes this in *Recovery, the Sacred Art: The Twelve Steps as Spiritual Practice*:

> The fundamental and paradoxical premise of the Twelve Step recovery as I experience it is this: The more clearly you realize your lack of control, the more powerless you discover yourself to be . . . (and) the more natural it is for you to be surrendered to God. . . . Radical powerlessness is radical freedom, liberating you from the need to control the ocean of life and freeing you to learn how best to navigate it.

In one of his April 2023 daily meditations from the Center for Action and Contemplation, Richard Rohr writes, "All great spirituality is about letting go. Instead, we have made it to be about taking in, attaining, performing, winning, and succeeding." A stance of relinquishment is the portal to the movement from control to trust. Though often ignored or explained away, it's what was taught and demonstrated by Jesus.

Jesus teaches that when a grain of wheat dies, it bears much fruit (Jn 12:24). He insists that if you try to hang on to your life, you will lose it (Mt 16:25). He asks what it profits you to gain the whole world but lose your soul (Mk 8:36). His words and parables point to a pattern of letting go of control, instead of clinging to your prerogatives, as the pathway to a fulfilled life.

The early church seemed to understand this pattern. The letter to those in Philippi tells them to "do nothing from selfish ambition or conceit," urging them to look "not to your own interests, but to the interests of others" (Phil 2:3–4). In that way they are to mirror the self-emptying love of Christ.

The gospel points to the imperative of relinquishing an egocentric self that thrives on confidence to conquer and control. That's what you must let go of to salvage your soul. And this is a spiritual struggle. It doesn't mean denying your gifts, abandoning your good work for just causes, or forgetting your service to the marginalized and to the church. The task is to learn how to place your trust in grace—grace that is sufficient—and find your life mysteriously upheld in the ocean of God's love. Only then will you become truly free to give yourself, with selfless abandon, to joining in God's work of healing the pain of the world.

There are dramatic examples of relinquishing control as a spiritual discipline. A favorite story comes from 891 in Ireland, when three monks, Dubslane, Macbeth, and Maelinmun, set off from the Irish coast purposely in a boat without oars. In a tradition of pilgrimage at that time, they were "wandering for the love of God," convinced they would be taken by spirit and wind to an intended destination. (They ended up in Cornwall, England.) Author and poet Christine Valters Painter describes this practice in a Patheos blog:

> In the tradition of Celtic monasticism, a very unique practice of pilgrimage arose called *peregrinatio*. The Irish monks would set sail in a small boat called a coracle, without oar or rudder, and let the winds and current of divine love carry them to the "place of their resurrection." . . . The impulse for the journey was always love. . . . This metaphor for journeying was a powerful one that shaped much of their vision of the way of the Christian spiritual life. *Peregrinatio* was the call to wander for the love of God. It is a word without precise definition in English and is a very particular kind of pilgrimage rooted in a willingness to yield to holy direction. This wandering was an invitation

into letting go of our own agendas and discovering where God was leading.

A boat without oars seems not just impractical, but reckless and foolish. Yet it's a metaphor for detaching your trust in the usual "oars" you use to gain mastery, control, and self-direction over how you live. Meister Eckhart, a prominent theologian, preacher, and monastic leader in the early fourteenth century, said this in one of his sermons: "God asks only that you get out of God's way and let God be God in you." That expresses the inward motivation of monks casting off in a boat without oars and captures in this way the dynamic of the movement from control to trust.

In *Crisis Contemplation: Healing the Wounded Village*, Barbara Holmes describes how external events can destroy your faith in mastery:

> If life, as we experience it, is a fragile crystal orb that holds our daily routines and dreams of order and stability, then sudden and catastrophic crises shatter this illusion of normalcy. The crises . . . are usually precipitated by circumstances beyond the ordinary. I am referring to oppression, violence, pandemics, abuses of power, or natural disasters and planetary disturbances.

In the midst of such times of crisis, Holmes says, you're given a way forward:

> We can journey inward, with or without music, with our bodies as engaged as our minds, but we must relinquish control and seek grounding within the mystical depths of inner spaces.

That's when you must refocus your attention. You can put into place external disciplines, structures, and practices that will provide the internal space required to live with a relinquished spirit that can navigate and rest in the ocean of God's love. But be clear about what this means, and what this doesn't mean. When David Whyte says so wisely, "What you can plan is too small for you to live," that doesn't mean you stop any planning. Daily you must plan to secure funds or meet the needs of organizations or diverse communities. But your true life can't be conscripted by your necessary planning.

How Structure Can Bring Freedom

The irony is that it will require plans and structures to detach you from your addictive belief in your control. Look again at the example of AA. The Twelve Step process provides a structure creating the space for one's inner life to move from the illusion of control to the truth of relinquishment, and then the pathway of liberation. The AA participant must plan to attend meetings that become the key environment where his or her holding space is strengthened and held in community.

Even more, consider life in a monastic community. Days are heavily structured, with regular gatherings of communal prayer, often five or more times beginning in the early morning and concluding just before sleep. Meals are often in silence, with readings. A well-planned, repetitive rhythm of prayer, work, and rest provides the external frame of each day. This is done to create and nurture the internal space in each monk's journey to relinquish egocentric habits of being and embrace a soul-centric life. Chanted psalms become the internal narration of this movement.

Certain structures are aimed at bringing you freedom. Those kinds of structure open space in both your internal life and your external activities. You will need to discover what kind of spiritual disciplines you'll need to discover or create an infrastructure that will slowly but surely free you from your obsessive desire to control your own destiny.

Keep in mind that you won't be able to support your spiritual infrastructure, and hold your holding space, on your own. Depending upon your temperament, personality type, and experience, searching for the right balance between what you internalize as ingrained soulful practices, and what is reinforced through communities and relationships that provide reliable accountability will be key. The examples of AA and monastic communities, plus many others, offer membership in a group with rigorous expectations that reinforce a daily pattern of life designed to liberate your inward journey. There are also other alternatives that require internal initiative and commitment, including intentional small groups, spiritual directors, regular retreats, and repetitive spiritual exercises using online tools that provide you with support and accountability.

Your needs will also likely change during your journey. But part of relinquishing control is being aware that you were intended for community: you can never do this kind of work alone.

Preserving this space where a disposition of trust has room to grow is the aim. This is how you develop a wellspring of spiritual resilience. That's what you will come to long for, like a deer panting for water. You will discover that resilience rather than control is your way forward. That's the embedded truth in the line from David Whyte. Overconfident plans of management are too small. Life overwhelms them and will overwhelm your soul without disciplines that build spiritual resilience.

The Painful Path of Relinquishment

What then will happen when you commit to some structure that will open this space? Over time, your desire for mastery and control will dissolve into relinquishment. That's the initial experience when you lay aside the oars that have felt glued to your hands. It is what needs to happen if you are determined to embark on your inward journey. Any movement from control to trust first encounters this disarming and something frightening call to relinquishment.

Ilia Delio is a Franciscan scientist, theologian, and author. Her work in science and religion has been award winning. But her insights also probe deeply into the nature of our spiritual journey. In *The Hours of the Universe; Reflections on God, Science, and the Human Journey* she describes with discerning wisdom:

> We must travel inward, into the interior depth of the soul where the field of divine love is expressed in the "thisness" of our own, particular life. . . . The journey inward requires surrender to this mystery in our lives, and this means letting go of our "control buttons." It means dying to the untethered selves that occupy us daily; it means embracing the sufferings of our lives, from the little sufferings to the big ones; it means allowing God's grace to heal us, hold us, and empower us for life. . . . It means being willing to surrender all that we have for all that we can become in God's love.

Letting go of control doesn't ease you into some relaxed state of nirvana. The inward journey you embrace more likely will uncover the sufferings often repressed by layers of protective dross—as well as sensitivity to the suffering of others. And there's some irony here. Richard Rohr, who often refers to Delio's work, has a unique definition of suffering. He describes it as "whenever we are not in control." Reflect on that for a few minutes. Moving from control to trust necessarily involves suffering. Relinquishment means acceptance of this.

Such suffering may come from wounds embedded deep within, which now you have the courage and insight to face.

Or it may be suffering imposed externally, through a tragic loss, betrayal, illness, catastrophe, or death. Or a suffering with those who suffer as we face the truth that we can't control the suffering of others. But to open any hope for healing through a longed-for presence of God's love, you will have to accept the relinquishment of your control.

Mature spirituality that embraces this truth with psychological realism rather than pietistic platitudes is hard to come by within the popular, prevailing propaganda of self-improvement. But you can find resources of wisdom, both ancient and modern, at times in unexpected places. In a thin blue pamphlet that has been nestled for five decades in a protected place on our bookshelf, I recently rediscovered Gordon Cosby's series of compiled sermons, "The Calling Forth of the Charisma." Cosby understood deeply how the emergence of your true self through the power of the Holy Spirit passes through a portal of pain. He describes how relinquishment exposes inner wounds that have repressed the gift of your true self:

> The real character of the new humanity is obscured for a time by the turmoil, the anxiety, the hostility, the downright hatred which also begin to emerge into consciousness. . . . This can be a time of discouragement and even despair, when one sees with great objectivity the unbelievable demonic dimensions of one's life, the indifference to the spiritual, one's unwillingness to take the risk of faith, one's

inability to love, and the ease with which we actually despise our brethren and call them fools in a thousand subtle ways. But even so, the new begins to emerge, and this "becoming" self is the gift of the Holy Spirit.

Three quarters of a century ago, Paul Tillich, the famous Protestant theologian who fled Germany and became highly influential in mainstream Protestantism and beyond, preached and wrote in *The Shaking of the Foundations*:

There is no excuse which permits us to avoid the depth of truth, the only way to which lies through the depth of suffering. Whether the suffering comes from outside and we take it upon ourselves as the road to the depth, or whether it be chosen voluntarily as the only way to deep things; whether it be the way of humility, or the way of revolution; whether the Cross be internal, or whether it be external, the road runs contrary to the way we formerly lived and thought. That is why Isaiah praises Israel, the Servant of God, in the depths of its suffering; and why Jesus calls those blessed who are in the depth of sorrow and persecution, of hunger and thirst in both body and spirit; and why He demands the loss of our lives for the sake of our lives.

The Deconstruction of Dreams

Your addiction to control, particularly if you are a social activist or organizational leader, may also get broken through painful realities that destroy your dreams and commitments. You're one, most likely, who is committed to making a difference in the world, a difference that is aligned with God's justice embodied within the beloved community. And you may be pouring your life into that quest. Perhaps, however, you've already discovered that the depth and fervency of your commitment cannot control the outcome. If not yet, at some point this is likely to be your devastating experience. You may be forced into relinquishment, and the suffering that this might entail. At that point you will want to discover if you have been thrown into a pit of despair or propelled into a portal of transformation.

One of the pivotal times when I experienced the deconstruction of my dreams, revealing the futility of my compulsion to control events, came when Kaarin and I abandoned our life in DC, including our life in the Sojourners community. During this time in the 1970s, a handful of radical Christian communities were emerging as an alternative model of the church. Sojourners embodied that vision, and I had been captivated by that calling. I began stepping away from Capitol Hill and my work with Senator Mark Hatfield, joining Jim Wallis as associate editor of *Sojourners* magazine. Kaarin and I, our marriage in its infancy, were moving toward being part of the Sojourners community. But we also had to navigate the differences in our callings. I was drawn to the vision of the intentional Christian community which Wallis and his companions were committed to founding. Kaarin had a far different response to the community. She felt an air of authoritarianism and judgment in the style of this community that triggered nerves from her past and felt a lack of acceptance for who she was at her core. Various interactions confirmed her fears. Trust in the community's way of living out its vision began eroding.

My energy was flowing into writing about the radical call of the gospel around the issues of war, violence, economic injustice, racial oppression, and more. I felt that the response had to be rooted in the life and witness of faithful Christian communities. This message was carried not only in print but at conferences, retreats, workshops, and sermons.

But inwardly my life was becoming arid. My energy was flowing in one direction only, into my outward journey. Moreover, the Sojourners community and its magazine, now absorbing my vocational energy, was proclaiming the radical difference the outward journey of following Christ could make against the world's oppressive structures and injustices. Alternative communities of faith that overcame individualism and found guidance corporately, through communal mutual submission, would lead the way. This was not an environment that nurtured or even welcomed the inward contemplative journey.

Prior to this, faith in my ability to live unto myself, with clever, subconscious defenses protecting me from vulnerable commitment to others, had been mercifully deconstructed. A thirst for belonging had emerged, found in silence before God, and then discovered in marriage as a gift that we were learning to preserve and nurture. But the insistent expectations of an alternative community, and the passion for a voice of radical social witness, ended up stalling and subverting the interior grounding of my soul.

Painful clarity came when we left Sojourners and our life in DC behind, ruptured relationships in the wake. Grandiose dreams of transforming the church, building a rarified, radical Christian community, and proclaiming a prophetic voice that could penetrate the corridors of power were all now in desolation. Words scribbled in my journal were a confessional lament:

<u>November 1, 1979, age 34</u>
Can I live without my dreams? And then might God grant their fulfillment?

My sense is that now is the time to relinquish all in order to discover my love for God. . . . To be set free from all else. So, no agenda. No place where I need to be.

To be where God can create what God's intention is. And to be where Kaarin and I are free to discover more deeply our love. That seems primary right now.

It is this utter relinquishment of agendas that seems to be the most critical thing to deal with for me now.

It is a contrite heart which God wants to give me. The wax must be soft.

The deconstruction of the dream embodied in my relationship to Sojourners, which I tried to embrace when leaving my work with Senator Mark Hatfield, proved to be one of the most painful times in the first half of my life. Yet, going through that pain and suffering was indispensable for opening, in time, the possibilities of vocational clarity, service, and ecumenical ministry that I never could have imagined.

Kaarin and I sought refuge in Missoula, Montana. This created a space, now unencumbered by the pretentious externalities of my life in DC, for a refining inner journey to continue. But it almost felt like starting over.

> January 18, 1980, age 34
> *I must begin the journey inwardly that I have just ended geographically. So hard it is to embark once again. Everything seems so dry, so distant.*
>
> *But I am here to discover what God has in store for me, for my life, for his creation in me. To reconnect with my spiritual identity.*
>
> *I hardly know how to begin.*

This wasn't the only time that I was confronted with the necessity to relinquish control in the face of deconstructed dreams. But it was the first and most formative one. Decades later the inner truths it uncovered still resonate. That's why I am sharing it with you. If you're in the early stages of your determined journey seeking the radical changes essential for our society and world, I hope a similar experience happens to you sooner rather than later.

That will sound strange, I know. I don't wish the experiences of suffering and desolation that come from deconstructed dreams on anyone. But I do wish for discerning wisdom and unbounded trust to grow in your life. You will need that if urgent, impassioned work is to evolve into a sustainable, indefatigable commitment of a lifetime.

Earlier I wrote that the journey toward an integrated, authentic, surrendered life won't be a steady, upward movement of one success building on another. Rather, each of the four movements you may discover in the quiet quest of your soul will go from secure *order*, through painful and shattering *disorder*, and then into transforming *reorder*, to use Richard Rohr's terms. It's another way of talking about life, death, and resurrection not as an abstract creed, but an experiential pathway revealing the Way revealed in Jesus, describing God's presence and grace at the foundation of all life. This trajectory, centered in the redeeming power of God's love in Jesus Christ, is seen in the life cycle of an insect, in the emergence of galaxies, and in the pilgrimage opening before you from a protected to a surrendered life.

Beckoned to Live in Trust

What happens when your reliance on control is shattered into the disorder of relinquishment? You are beckoned toward trust. This is trust that is not a slogan or a doctrine, but a radical disposition of your life. It comes as you experience being enveloped by a Presence far beyond your ability to control. The deconstructing weight of relinquishment is converted into a gift and a portal for your transformation. This trust helps you discover how to abide in love as a vine abides in a branch.

Such trust invites your detachment from the immediate outcomes of your efforts. For the committed social activist, as much as for a college president, priest, or congregational pastor, this seems counter-intuitive. And it is. You are probably riveted to a cause-and-effect framework for evaluating your actions. Governing boards, foundations, donors, and congregational members will hold you accountable for the concrete outcomes of what you do. All this is understandable and requires your attention.

What happens when your reliance on control is shattered into the disorder of relinquishment? You are beckoned toward trust.

But that common framework of thinking and evaluating your actions used by others, and probably internalized by you, has three shortcomings. First, it functions on a narrow and circumscribed time frame, assuming that immediate results are what really matter. But the deep changes needed and desired require "urgent patience" over an expanded time. Second, this mindset vastly overestimates the efficacy of your plans and strategies and dangerously underestimates the impact of events and forces beyond your control. Third, this framework makes it tempting for you to utilize any means possible, including those that may violate basic values, to try to achieve the outcomes desired. But as Gandhi said, "The means are the end in the making."

Theologically, what is at stake here is your understanding of God. The dominant framework of seeking control through reliance on a cause-and-effect understanding of outcomes diminishes God. Your God becomes too small. Your movement from control through relinquishment to trust is facilitated by an expanding view of God's mysterious, pervasive, sustaining presence in all of creation, holding together all things, including the center and future of your life. That gift of trust is the only way to embrace this grace.

What is it like to experience this, even for brief moments? Think of a hitter in baseball who stops thinking about his grip, or his stance, or his swing, and even stops trying to second guess what the pitcher is going to throw. He's just present to the moment, without self-consciousness, and swings the way he knows how, effortlessly, free from fear, doubt, worry about results, and over-thinking, simply totally present to this moment. Or listen to an artist describing being carried forward with brush strokes transcending thoughts or plans, but charting a path of color on the color that coheres the painting. Poets and fiction writers share how in certain inspired moments the words flow with uninhibited energy as the piece seems to write itself.

Perhaps that's something like what you experience when you move beyond the calculated limitations of control to the creative vulnerability of trust. You surrender and connect to a subtle, flowing, empowering energy. There's a sense of Presence you connect to, and know it to be God's love. That's why, where, and how you can trust.

You can't predict and package your soul's disposition of trust. But the practices of your holding space will prepare you to welcome these times and even rest there. Let me describe for you glimpses of what this is like:

> March 30, 2007, age 62
> *Sister Laura, my spiritual director, told me this morning that "time for centering myself is my salvation."*
>
> *We talked about what I'd call the "mystery" of my leadership. Increasingly, I sense that I simply bring a presence, an openness, a sharing that comes more from the heart. . . . But for this to happen I have to keep nurturing my inner life. . . . There's a way in which my leadership style seems a lot less self-conscious. I just do what seems natural or right. And often I am genuinely surprised at the reaction of other people, when they are so affirming. It does feel that this is all beyond me, or that it's more than what I am doing. That's genuinely what makes this a "mystery."*
>
> *It's hard. I remember a poem about being carried in the flow of a river. . . . This image of a river of grace remains so intuitively powerful.*

Adam Bucko, an Episcopal priest involved in ministry with young people who are homeless, writes about how, for someone who is solution oriented, limitations and failures of the outcomes shattered his confidence and sent him into a crisis. Yet it pushed him toward something more intuitive and moved him toward deeper prayer. In his book *Let Your Heartbreak Be Your Guide: Lessons in Engaged Contemplation,* he writes:

> I started showing up for every person who needed my help in the same way that I was showing up for prayer. . . . I would just be there with homeless youth in a state of not knowing and trust. Paying attention to what was, bearing witness to their pain, helping them to hold their pain, and often breaking with them as a result of what I was witnessing. . . .
>
> What I began discovering is that every time I allowed myself to feel at a loss in the face of the pain I witnessed, every time I touched my own irrelevance, there was this energy of God that would begin to emerge in our midst. All I had to do was say yes to it. The presence of God was there, always ready to pick up the broken pieces from the floor and re-assemble them into something good. . . . When that happened, I realized that my skills were not useless. I just needed to first surrender them to God, so God could use them however God wished. So right words could come. So right ways of being present could manifest. . . . It was often not clear who was helping whom. Because in each of those

sacred moments I received just as much as I was giving, if not more.

These are some pictures of what it looks like to move from control through relinquishment into a posture of trust. Your experience will be shaped by elements unique to your journey and personality traits intrinsic to the tapestry of your strengths and vulnerabilities. But the broad strokes of this movement seem common to all on the journey. You'll find that trust often seems to be moving in the darkness without touch points that provide some measure of security. But at times light breaks through, unexpectedly, in ways that will reassure you that your soul is finding its home.

The Final Letting Go

The movement from control through relinquishment into trust is your preparation for the final step in the journey of your life, namely, your death. That's the ultimate challenge of letting go, surrendering your mastery over your destiny, embracing the suffering of relinquishment, and finding trust and peace in the nearer Presence of God enveloping your soul. It's common to ponder this final stage when age, at least statistically, brings you closer to life's completion. But at any age, confronting your eventual death can be a liberating avenue that recenters your soul in trust and grace rather than in anxious compulsions of control. The sooner this happens in your journey, the freer you will be fearlessly to follow God's call.

You should learn to "die" before you die if you are to live and serve with abandon. When you reflect on those personalities whose work for God's justice, liberation, and the flourishing of all life have left an imprint on history, you can sense how they freed themselves from the preoccupation with their ego, from the glorification of their power, from their drive to control. That's part of what died as their inward journey ushered them into an expansive trust in the mystery of God's love. Julian of Norwich. St. Francis of Assisi. John Wesley. Mahatma Gandhi. Martin Luther King, Jr. Dorothy Day. Dag Hammarskjöld. So many more. It's not simply that they had overcome fear of their physical death at life's end. Rather, they were finding liberation from the power of death that opened their life to trust in God's love in the present moment, and for the world's future. This is not just a rarified experience for saints. It is also accessible to you.

If you find yourself in the early phases of your vocational calling and outward activism for causes that compel your response, you may be captivated by your sense of agency. As you discover your gifts and learn how your actions can make an impact, you probably feel flowing energy and power that propel you forward. Often those whose witness and work are thriving in these ways may feel nearly invincible and free of limitations. That may have characterized your approach to your outward journey in the first years of engagement in witness, work, and action.

Perhaps because you are on a "high" of seeming invulnerability, you feel consciously immune to the specter of failure, disillusionment, desolation, and death. But even though repressed from your mental awareness, those realities can haunt your soul. And when they are not acknowledged and recognized, their subtle power increases. At times those fears and dread can erupt into the surface, suddenly paralyzing your feelings.

In the first half of my life I encountered such experiences, at times in what seemed like the mostly unlikely circumstances. In 1974, as the Vietnam war had finally wound down, Senator Hatfield turned his attention to addressing world hunger. In November he was part of the US delegation to the UN World Food Conference in Rome, and I accompanied him as his principal aide. At twenty-nine years of age, I was interacting with diplomats as well as advocacy groups from around the world trying to meet a humanitarian crisis. It felt awesome. But then I had a startling apprehension:

NOVEMBER 6, 1974, AGE 29
I had been in prayer and meditation when the fear of death suddenly seized my soul. The chill of knowing the inevitable. It is irrational, absurd, and my spirit rebels with protective defiance—to cling to my existence and all that is me; never to give it up.

But that is the gravest power of Death—to refuse the relinquishment of one's being, for therein is the "pride of life" which breeds Death in all our acts. . . .

All the mystics, who probe the unknown caverns of the interior terrain, discover the love that flows forth at the

> *root of Being. They encounter love; love rests at the heart. To be in its flow is life. . . .*
>
> *Death is overcome when we lose ourselves in love, as love flows out for others.*
>
> *That is liberation.*

The fear of death might unexpectedly impinge into your consciousness in this way when you are younger and vital. In fact, research has shown that the fear of death is often experienced strongly by men and women in their twenties, and then begins to recede. For women, however, although not for men, one study showed, this fear often escalates again in their fifties. There's even a clinical name for a strong, intense fear of death: *thanatophobia*. Look this up, and you'll see in the list that the primary cause of this phobia is fear of losing control.

Some studies show that those who are elderly are likely to fear the process of dying more than death itself. Facing your death is the most challenging and yet potentially the most liberating step in your movement from control through relinquishment to trust. There is no exit from your physical destiny. Your holding space should free your deepest self to embrace the relinquishing of your physical life through an embedded trust in God's love upholding and energizing the center of all that is. When your soul is ready for this, at any age, your life can be surrendered to join the transforming, healing power of this love active in the world.

J￼ULY 19, 2017, AGE 72

At this stage of my life, at 72, dealing with aging—knees, back, prostate—this is true at a physical level. My body will begin to impose some limitations. And so I need to surrender control in that sense. And this is the direction, this is the end. This is the final destination—the complete surrender of all control to God. To only be in God's presence, at death, and then the life that endures. So living in this posture of surrender now begins to prepare the way.

In a mysterious inward rhythm, relinquishment in the face of the abyss of nothingness draws us into full communion. On your inward and outward journey, if you've honed your attentiveness in the practices of your holding space, you'll catch glimpses and glimmerings of this when the center of all life breaks through and touches you, as a sign that it can engulf you.

When you reach that final time when any and all yearning for control has ended, the imprint of repetitive and even daily practices of surrender can carry you in a pervasive trust that overflows the boundaries of your life into that Love that is the center of all life.

Facing your death is the most challenging and yet potentially the most liberating step in your movement from control through relinquishment to trust.

VIII.

Gathered Wisdom

Michael Goldhaber saw it coming. Formerly a theoretical physicist, as early as the mid-1980s he perceived that people were having more access to information through the internet and the web than they could possibly deal with. What matters, he maintained in a *New York Times* opinion piece, is where you and I give our attention. And since the object of this attention is discretionary, intense pressures arise to capture your attention, creating what Goldhaber calls "the attention economy." Today, high-tech firms are in intense competition to attract and keep your attention, which galvanizes you to your mobile devices. And it creates a lot of noise. Those decibels invariably silence other voices, but they also silence our own, making it harder to discern, if you're young, your sense of calling. If you've been in justice and advocacy work for a while, they often drown out your ability to listen for the quiet wisdom that points you to next steps.

The initial and perhaps most persistent obstacle to constructing your holding space is your mental distraction. This seems to bedevil every attempt to center yourself, to pray, to be silent, to be still and open to your surroundings, to write in your journal, and simply to listen for God's voice and sense God's presence.

Ruth Haley Barton, in *Sacred Rhythms: Arranging Our Lives for Spiritual Transformation,* shows great perception as she describes the process of discernment:

> The habit of discernment is a quality of attentiveness to God that is so intimate that over time we develop an intuitive sense of God's heart and purpose in any given moment. We become familiar with God's voice—the tone, quality and content—just as we become familiar with the voice of a human being we know well. We are able to grasp the answers to several key questions: Who is God for me in the moment? Where is God at work, continuing to unfold . . . love and redemption? Who am I most authentically in response?

But when can you say you have gotten there? And why does it seem so difficult to hold yourself in your holding space in the noise of news, social media, the internet?

Howard Rheingold, who has written widely about social media, developments in technology, and their effects on the mind, puts it this way: "Attention is a limited resource, so pay attention to where you pay attention." You are living in the first generation that has potentially unlimited access to information and experiences about everything, with its delivery augmented in speed, efficiency, and comprehensiveness by artificial intelligence. The only limitation is determined by what you impose, whether consciously or unconsciously. And your choices should be intentional. This requires an internal grounding sustained by your holding space.

And while the technological environment curating information has changed dramatically, the spiritual challenge of dealing with the distracted mind is ancient. Jamie Kreiner has written a remarkable book, *The Wandering Mind: What Medieval Monks Tell about Distraction,* which explores with scholarly comprehensiveness the numerous ways monastic leaders and their communities addressed mental distraction in their contemplative practices over hundreds of years. As Kreiner explains:

> Distractedness was a kind of preexisting condition—internal, nonconscious, and entangled with the self—that compromised the very commitment to concentrating on things that were important and good. For many Christian monks, distraction wasn't just a potential interference. It had already breached the walls and made itself at home.

Monastic leaders like theologian John Cassian, writing in the early fifth century, knew that mental distraction had to be challenged at its roots. He traveled widely to discover monastic best practices. As Kreiner explains, Cassian analyzed distraction fifteen-hundred years ago in ways that probably resonate with you, as with me:

> It [distraction] had also come to signal underlying cognitive conditions that could afflict even people

who were determined to think and act ethically. And because it stemmed from inner turmoil, it could not be corrected simply by avoiding certain stimuli or by resolving to have better intentions or practices. Monks had to tackle distraction systemically, and they saw it as their moral responsibility to do so. If we feel the same way, that's in part thanks to early Christian monasticism.

Most likely you have no interest or intention of retreating into a monastery or the desert. Whatever your situation, the invitation here is to discover how to become inwardly set apart. The most important dimension is discovering how you create detachment from the cultural conditioning that has quietly but pervasively captured your mind and wants to own your soul. That is what you begin to dismantle as you diminish the power of mental distraction, becoming ever more vulnerable to God's presence in your life and attentive to the continuing invasion of God's suffering love into the heart of the world's pain and brokenness.

Some form of community will be essential as you are on the journey from the protected life to the surrendered life through each of the four movements we have explored. You can investigate forms of the new monasticism beginning to emerge. Those yearning for a transformative inward spiritual experience often are looking for ways to incorporate features of monastic practices within their daily lives, vocational commitments, marriages, and families. This can take root with emerging forms of worshipping communities, house churches, small groups, retreats, and other gatherings. And discovering and building communities like this will prevent your inward journey from being victimized by the hyper-individualism pervading our culture.

What Difference Will Your Holding Space Make?

Maybe you are stymied by the monks and feel there's a kind of rarified air they breathe, wondering, "What's the point?" But perhaps your curiosity is aroused by descriptions of what your inward journey could reveal and entail if it were seriously embraced. And maybe you've begun to imagine what each of the four movements would look like in practice in your own life's journey. Still, you may wonder whether it all is worth the effort. Is this all a privileged excursion into a privatized spirituality that actually deflects attention and saps energy from addressing the overbearing injustices that afflict the world, posing threats to survival of the most vulnerable among us and to our planetary home?

You're right to ask that question. And you need to discover a compelling answer. Whatever your starting place (wisdom from the monks, or a quiet stillness that calls you in nature), it's important to have a sustained holding space. And a holding space will require acquiring new habits, undertaking practices that take repetition to learn well, the same way physical exercises develop muscle memory. You will need an inner assurance that this opens you to the love and work of God in your life and in the world.

What you will experience through a holding space that makes room for contemplative journey is the vision to see reality clearly, in focus. You will see through all the external, distracting clutter into the heart of things. That includes the realities of your own life, that of others, the foundation of the world's life, and the signs of God's presence in and through all. Parker Palmer in *The Active Life: A Spirituality of Work, Creativity, and Caring,* puts it this way: "The function of contemplation in all its forms is to penetrate illusion and help us touch reality."

Don't underestimate the ubiquitous presence of cultural, political, social, and even religious clutter to obscure your vision. The world of politics, for instance, normally absorbs your attention through its dynamics of power and money, with the competing drives of egocentric ambition often reinforced by deceit. Devotion by politicians to the common good is increasingly uncommon. It takes detachment to see beyond the corrosive, self-referential, embedded patterns of political behavior to reveal deeper truths. And it requires a contemplative perspective to envision political action that finds its starting point as the reach of God's love present to all people and embedded in all creation, offering redemptive promise in the face of suffering and destruction.

Finding how you can focus a clearer vision that grasps the core of reality more truly, with detachment from immediate distractions, is a key, foundational step forward. This is clearly illustrated in the old saying about not seeing the forest for the trees.

Prophets always have the gift of seeing things clearly, unmasking and revealing reality. In the life of the people of Israel the prophets delivered incisive words of judgment and social critique because they saw through the illusions of privileged comfort and exclusionary self-righteousness that prevented the religious and political establishment from hearing the call of God's judgment, repentance and promise.

The power to break through those barricades came from the prophets' own encounters with the living God, allowing them to deliver what they confidently proclaimed as the word of the Lord. This same power was fully revealed in the life of Jesus, who began his public ministry by proclaiming words from Isaiah, "The Spirit of the Lord is upon me" (Lk 4:18).

One way to think about your calling, nurtured and sustained through the practices of your holding space, is this biblical integration of prophecy and mysticism. Albert Nolan, a South African Catholic priest who became a leading theological voice in the anti-apartheid movement, writes this in his influential book *Jesus Today: A Spirituality of Radical Freedom:*

> Traditionally . . . prophets were mystics and mystics were prophets. Any idea that one could be a prophet calling for justice and social change without some experience of union with God was unthinkable. Equally unthinkable was any idea that one could be a perfectly good mystic without becoming critically outspoken about the injustices of one's time.

That's the bedrock of the difference made when you ground your work for justice in the journey of your soul. Charles Péguy, a French poet and writer who worked in solidarity with workers and peasants, put it this way over a century ago: "Everything begins in mysticism and ends in politics."

Eight Roots to Ground Your Action for Justice

An inward grounding should make a practical difference in your political engagement, social action, and outward witness. Your vision, starting point, and disposition will bear distinctive features. I'd invite you to consider at least eight ways this may be evidenced. You may have others to add.

1. You Know This World Belongs to God

The extremes on the religious right and the secular left share a common assumption that this world is controlled by hostile, evil forces. Fundamentalist religion is convinced that the "world" is hopelessly headed for divine judgment and destruction preceding God's eternal rule. Some extreme factions from Christian as well as other religious traditions believe that the righteous, violent actions of a committed minority against reigning worldly powers will be God's instrument to hasten divine vengeance and judgment, creating a purified social order.

Fundamentalists on the secular left define the world as in the grip of oppressive forces that, if not successfully resisted, will result in accelerated human destruction and planetary collapse. Militarism, racism, patriarchy, authoritarianism, neocolonialism, and classism have corrupted the world to its core. Religion, at best, is an intoxicating diversion from reality, and often a sanctifying rationale for brutality. The struggle for survival requires fierce opposition, through any effective means, to the world's oppressive powers.

These starting points begin with a binary view of reality, dividing the world into clear demarcations of good and evil. Certainty and self-righteousness become nearly absolute, opposed to an evil world with leaders and their followers who are demonized religiously or politically.

But you are offered a different starting point. You can begin with the clear conviction that this world belongs to God. This is the deepest truth about our planetary home and all who live here. All of life is permeated and upheld by the presence and breath of God. This world is beloved by its Creator, precious to its core. You start by knowing, beyond knowledge, that you live in the midst of limitless love desiring to shape the essence of the world's life.

None of this minimizes the gravity of the threats to human flourishing and planetary sustainability. As said, the prophetic call unveils realities that are denied or minimized to our peril. The catastrophic unraveling of the climate's sustainability; the accelerating inequity of income; the unmitigated ravages of several wars; the entrenched systems of racial, cultural, and political oppression; and so much more afflict God's world. Your witness should always embrace and announce these threats. It's the roots of your response, however, that makes all the difference.

The grounding of your life, at the center of your being, in God's expansive love connects you to God's beloved embrace of the world. As you move from life protected by your self-sufficiency to a life surrendered in belonging to God, you participate in the flow of love through which the whole world belongs to God. From that starting point you confront the evil that besieges the world. From that assurance you shape a compelling vision of a future embedded in the intentions of the world's Creator and Lover. From that conviction of faith you can be sustained by a hope that truly does conquer fear.

2. Your Engagement with the World Has a Spiritual Foundation

If you have been involved in any movement seeking fundamental social change involving justice, peace, climate protection, human rights, or similar causes, you've recognized that the challenges being confronted have economic, political, and social dimensions. Economic power supporting the status quo must be restrained and realigned. Laws need to be changed. Leaders with trustworthy commitments need to gain political office. Civil society should be emboldened to strengthen social movements. Social norms require transformation.

All these dimensions of change are essential. Any analysis of major social movements, such as the civil rights struggle, antiwar efforts, the women's movement, human rights campaigns, and international climate-justice advocacy require economic, political, and social action. Yet, if you are a contemplative and a prophet, you know that there is more involved.

The forces enshrining injustice, brutal military violence, climate destruction, and the violation of human dignity have a corporate spiritual dimension. Their hold reaches into the hearts and minds of those wielding power. Idolatry, which is the worship of false gods, claims zealous allegiance from those who benefit and defend that status quo. This is what the New Testament means when it warns that we "wrestle not against flesh and blood, but against principalities, against powers, against the rulers of the darkness of this world, against spiritual wickedness in high places" (Eph 6:12).

Rahiel Tesfamariam, a social activist born in Eritrea who immigrated as a child to the United States, received a master of divinity degree from Yale and is a leader in present civil rights struggles. She is the author of *Imagine Freedom: Transforming Pain into Political and Spiritual Power*. In a 2024 interview with *Sojourners* magazine, she shared this:

> We don't often look at white supremacy as a form of spiritual warfare against us, one that we must arm ourselves against and resist. It's not just a system; it's also a spiritual war. . . .
>
> We always thought power was about who we put into office. . . . We are living in a moment when we can have all that in place, have all the ducks lined up—even have the "right party" in place—and still we see some of the worst acts of

> brutality ever witnessed with our own eyes. Then you get to a place where you say, maybe it's not about political power. Maybe it's about giving the enemy power over our souls. It's not about which Pharaoh we pick. It's about whether or not Pharaoh is in our mind.

You need not make an either/or judgment about political change and spiritual transformation. But it's crucial to recognize that the movements for social change desperately needed for a liberating future include a radical transformation of values and attitudes that requires spiritual power. A holding space will prepare you for that level of engagement.

The late Desmond Tutu shared with audiences a story about meeting a nun who prayed for him and the anti-apartheid struggle every night. "Hey, here I am being prayed for by a nun at 2 am in the woods in California," Tutu proclaimed. "What chance does the South African apartheid government stand?" Whether you are praying in the middle of the night or being arrested for a nonviolent sit-in at the Capitol for climate justice, your inward spiritual engagement and outward witness should be woven together seamlessly.

3. *You Act on the Basis of Call*

A prophetic view of reality, breaking through superficial illusions, reveals the depth and the breadth of the world's wounds and brokenness demanding attention. Calls to action addressing urgent causes resound and rebound within spaces devoted to social change and justice. When you are open to act, whether giving money, doing volunteer work, serving on a board, joining a demonstration, or redirecting your vocational life, the options suddenly are endless, and all of them seem equally imperative. How do you decide what to do?

My early pilgrimage, as I've shared, was shaped by belonging to Church of the Saviour in Washington, DC. There I first heard the language about acting in response to "call." The expectation was that a disciplined inward journey would result in clarity about where your outward work and witness should be directed. This would emerge as you began to hear God's call. That call might first sound like an impossible or impractical goal, like providing shelter for those homeless and afflicted with AIDS, or establishing a health clinic providing integrated physical, psychological, and spiritual care, or providing a committed Christian community and gainful employment for all those reentering society from DC's local prisons.

> *When you are open to act, whether giving money, doing volunteer work, serving on a board, joining a demonstration, or redirecting your vocational life, the options suddenly are endless, and all of them seem equally imperative. How do you decide what to do?*

In the broader church community I was in, when such a call was heard, it was held seriously and shared with the community, as others were invited to join if that call resonated deep within them. Then, a mission group would be formed of those beckoned to that outward call and committed to hold each other accountable to shared disciplines nurturing their inward journeys, their holding place.

Today there are over forty ministries and initiatives in the DC area, autonomously organized, that emerged from this communal process of listening to call and responding, all from a relatively small number of people in the groups and communities with roots in the Church of the Saviour and its legacy.

You will find it difficult, if not impossible, to prioritize the direction of your outward call by trying to decide what is most urgent. Constructing a hierarchy of urgency is a frustrating and ultimately futile way forward. Likewise, guiding your outward actions for justice and witness only on the basis of what makes strategic and tactical sense is not call. Often, the voice missing in the pragmatic debates about tactics of social change is a clarion call that holds forth the underlying goal of a movement. Rooted in your discernment of God's call on your life, yours can be such a voice.

Consider what it might be like to discover your outward journey, and the places where you pour out your energy, to emerge from an inner holding space that has allowed you to listen for and hear God's call. While organizing your social action and witness simply on the basis of what needs to be done will deplete you, you will learn that having a holding space roots your actions in your sincere efforts to discover God's call, which will center you with inner clarity and renewable energy.

4. Your Action Is Steadfast, Committed to the Long Term
Committed to social change, you want to see results. The urgency and threat of challenges to human livelihood and planetary survival plead for immediate and effective action. Timeframes of expectations become constricted, often riveted to election cycles. Yet to become focused on immediacy, you will experience frustration and even disillusionment when hoped-for results are not forthcoming within your range of expectations. The temptation then may be to give up in despair, or to move on to a different issue.

A holding space allowing your inward journey to strengthen its roots will alter your future horizon and liberate your expectations from pragmatic expediency. You'll acquire a healthy detachment from immediate efficacy. And that's crucial for strengthening the steadfastness of your commitment. If you are truly called by God to your outward journey, you are likely to be called toward goals that, in practical timelines, seem nearly impossible. That's because you're participating at some level in the work to bring about God's promised and preferred future for the world. And this coming reign of God's righteousness and love over all breaks into this world sporadically, and partially, often in unexpected places, like a stable for an unhoused couple giving birth. Yet its promise is completely trustworthy, evidenced in an empty tomb.

Your resolve and unshakable confidence in the holy significance of your action comes not from any short-term results that you may achieve, but from the attachment of your soul to the power of God's love for this world. That's why you cannot be shaken. That's how you will persevere through defeats. That's the way your work will serve as inspiring encouragement to others.

You will be there for the long term, with the necessary combination of urgency and patience. And that will bring realism to your indefatigable commitment. The truth is that deep social change, which alters history and moves the needle in the direction of justice, peace, integrity of creation, and equity, takes time. A lot of time. All historic and ongoing social movements demonstrate this. The abolition of slavery. The anti-colonial movements. The securing of civil rights for all. The empowerment of women with equal agency in society. The anti-apartheid movement. The end of torture. The establishment of international courts for crimes against humanity. The environmental movement. Global commitments to curtail climate change. Eliminating the death penalty. The abolition of nuclear weapons. The end to genocide. All these movements and many more, past and present, always stretch our horizon of the anticipated time to achieve them. And those remembered or honored today for providing leadership in those movements followed a call, held a vision, and kept steadfast.

5. *You Display Resilience*
Your commitment to change drives a need to control outcomes. That's natural. You are working to make a difference. So you work on devising the most effective strategies and developing ways to measure your results. If you apply and

receive grants from foundations to support your efforts, it's likely that they will impose requirements to report measurable, quantifiable outcomes as a condition for their support.

But when your goals are linked, explicitly or implicitly, to God's desired outcomes for a beloved world, and the building of a beloved community as an embodiment of that end, you see a bigger picture and know setbacks are inevitable. You're seeking deep change, which encompasses transforming values, altering attitudes, expanding expectations, and remaking cultures. Such radical change, imperative for ushering in fresh ways for human communities and the earth to flourish rather than perish, is not easily reduced to measurable, immediate quantifiable outcomes.

Earlier in the book we looked at prayer as detachment from the fruit of your actions. This is when that truth makes a critical difference. You don't need to rely on better strategies and more control over outcomes. Sure, you will always be attentive to the impact of what you do and search for creative, fresh paths toward your goals. But don't let your confidence become dependent on the standard measurements of success and failure. Your holding space should nurture a healthy detachment from the measurable achievements or shortcomings of your work. More is out of your control than you and others normally imagine.

Resilience is the most valuable gift you can offer to the movements and actions to which God has called you. Particularly in a time when political events and global trends create headwinds that threaten to overwhelm the prospects of crucial social change, your capacity to stay grounded and engaged with unquenchable hope is what will matter most. Here, your movement from control to trust in your inward journey will provide the wellspring for your outward engagement.

Here's an example you might find encouraging. In the city where Kaarin and I live, John Wester is the Catholic archbishop of the Archdiocese of Santa Fe, New Mexico. In 2017 he took a trip to Japan and visited Hiroshima and Nagasaki. Images from the peace memorials in those places left searing impressions on his heart. Returning home, he realized that his archdiocese is at the epicenter of the nuclear age—the place where the first atomic bomb was developed and detonated, and where the modernization of our massive nuclear arsenal continues.

Archbishop Wester felt called to enter the movement for nuclear disarmament, and he has become a key religious voice of leadership and witness. In 2022 he released a powerful and influential pastoral letter, "Living in the Light of Christ's Peace: A Conversation toward Nuclear Disarmament." The archbishop has worked with numerous groups and coalitions, including a partnership with four Catholic archdioceses—Hiroshima, Nagasaki, Seattle, and Santa Fe—working toward a world without nuclear weapons. In an address he gave to a Catholic Worker national gathering, Wester explained, "It's often said that pursuing disarmament is naive—but isn't it truly naive to think we can rely on luck to avoid nuclear catastrophe?"

Archbishop Wester has embarked on this outward witness and work after sensing God's call in response to his experiences. His goal, nothing less than the abolition of nuclear weapons, seems impossible. But it is rooted in God's intentions for this world. Wester's work, among all his other duties, remains steadfast. And he is not deterred by developments now increasing nuclear arsenals, but brings resilience in his witness, inspiring others. The archbishop has a holding space, a place of retreat at the same monastery in New Mexico that I love to visit. His witness may offer you an example of how a cultivated inward journey makes a decisive difference in an outward witness marked by ongoing resilience.

6. You Detach from Your Ego
As a person committed to making a difference in the lives of others, in local communities, and in the world, you are probably wired with a determined drive to achieve goals through your active engagement in causes. Others may even call you a strong leader. Persons like this, if they explore the Enneagram, discover that they often fit the profile of Type Eight, called the Challenger. The Enneagram Institute summarizes Type Eights in this way:

> Eights are self-confident, strong, and assertive. Protective, resourceful, straight-talking, and decisive, but can also be ego-centric and domineering. Eights feel they must control their environment,

especially people, sometimes becoming confrontational and intimidating. Eights typically have problems with their tempers and with allowing themselves to be vulnerable. At their Best: self-mastering, they use their strength to improve others' lives, becoming heroic, magnanimous, and inspiring.

When providing examples of Type Eight persons, the Institute lists Martin Luther King, Jr., Oskar Schindler, Winston Churchill, Fidel Castro, and Golda Meir, among many others. Those who lead movements often fall into this category, as do those who start churches. This also includes people who lead in different contexts; a stay-at-home dad chairing a church committee or a religious sister living in a cloistered community may also be Eights. Anyone fitting this profile is known for wanting to be in charge, to lead, and to make a mark, whether in the wider world or in their immediate community.

If you are an Eight, your most primitive fear is losing power and allowing anyone else to be in control. So you may act as a strong individualist, ready to defend yourself against hurt or rejection. The Institute points out that the struggle toward health or disintegration centers on whether or not you are highly egocentric. The Enneagram Institute states, "The more Eights build up their egos in order to protect themselves, the more sensitive they become to any real or imaginary slight to their self-respect, authority, or preeminence." Here, your movement from grandiosity to authenticity becomes crucial.

Whether or not you fit the specific characteristics of a Type Eight, if you are a change-maker, reformer, activist, community leader, pastor, or priest, your healthy detachment from an egocentric imprint on how you act and what you achieve is essential to serving as a transforming presence in your outward journey toward justice. In the end, it's not about you. Privately desiring to see your name in lights will dim the cause and calling you have discerned from God. So many gifted leaders, in my experience, lose their way because they haven't learned the spiritual and psychological pathway to separate their ego from the results of their efforts. Typically, they haven't acquired the courage and insight to recognize their shadow side, which is embedded within their extraordinary gifts. Unrecognized, it begins to infiltrate their inner self, which inevitably corrodes their outward actions.

> *So many gifted leaders . . . lose their way because they haven't learned the spiritual and psychological pathway to separate their ego from the results of their efforts.*

Your commitment to a holding space, with regular and well-curated spiritual practices including listening, and silence, will offer the opportunity to face and defuse the power of your shadow side. You'll be able to distill the fruits of your actions from the thirst of your ego. You will uncover your inner drives and motivations, facing them with courageous honesty.

Detaching these from ego enhancement requires a spiritual journey that deepens your relinquishment of your whole soul to God's presence and purposes.

And that will make a difference.

Others will trust you more deeply when they see that the heart of your focus for justice is faithfully and fearlessly riveted to God's transforming work in the world and not on mislaid attention on trying to portray your indispensable role in that process.

7. *You Don't Demonize Your Opponents*

One of the most difficult tasks you will face in your journey is to hold fast to the prophetic urgency of your call addressing specific points of the world's injustice while maintaining an open heart toward your opponents. Certainly, you've already encountered this. Our toxic and polarizing political and cultural environment only intensifies this challenge. And society's retreat into tribal enclaves expressed geographically, socially, and religiously, and reinforced by social-media bubbles, restricts the naturally occurring occasions requiring you to address this tension.

It's a challenge that drives deep into your inner self. When you feel hurt or offended, your natural instinct is to strike back in like manner. And when you face those with whom you don't just disagree, but whose power and influence is intensifying the suffering, exploitation, and injustice that you abhor, you feel compelled to denounce and condemn them. Feelings of hatred toward those you believe are inflicting their enmity and oppression on others lie close to the surface of your emotions, regardless of your public persona of spirituality. When justice, peace, and even planetary survival are at stake in the battle you're waging, your tendency will be to attack, humiliate, and defeat your opponents.

However, you've heard another voice, echoed in the words of biblical wisdom and exemplified in the witness of Jesus that says that this tempting trajectory of innate reactivity, of an eye for an eye, leads down a spiral of death. Neither hope nor change can flourish in a continuing recycle of mutual recrimination and vengeance. Radical, transforming change will only come when that cycle is broken. Yet that is no simple, conscious choice. It requires transforming, inner work that invites a breakthrough into a new way of embracing reality. Richard Rohr puts it this way in one of his daily meditations from the Center for Action and Contemplation:

> Unless we are led to some kind of contemplative practices that continually reveal our dualistic, argumentative, and biased ways of thinking, we won't move into a new stage of life. We'll just have opinions. What we really need is a sustained practice that rewires and transforms our hearts and minds.

The only hope you will have to become free from demonizing your opponents without curtailing in any way the strength and integrity of your witness and action is to participate in the embracing love of God, which sees the gold at the heart of the one whom you would hate. That image of God is there, even though it is covered with dross and buried beneath the consciousness of the other. You can only seek to reach out toward the intrinsic, divine worth of your ruthless opponent by experiencing how that same image is imprinted on your soul, beneath all your own dross.

Elizabeth Neuman, an expert on domestic terrorism, was asked at a conference how an extreme terrorist, committed to violence, can ever be changed. She shared how this had been studied extensively. And the process of potentially changing the mindset and violent actions of such a person typically begins when extreme empathy is extended to such a person from an unexpected source. When you demonize an opponent, you cancel any hope, however unlikely, of changing the person's convictions or establishing any basis of connection, even as your binary thinking gets reinforced and your opponent is permanently dehumanized as "the other."

Your holding space can open another path. Nothing is assured, of course. But when you live deeply into your true self, held as God's Beloved, your life can become a portal for grace and love to touch another in ways far beyond your conventional expectation.

8. You Are Rooted and Grounded in Love
The final way that your commitment to holding space can make a difference in your outward journey returns us to the starting question of this book: Where do you root your life?

It takes courage for you to ask that question honestly and intentionally. And this is the starting point on your journey, as you move from a self-protected life to a surrendered life through each of the movements of your soul that have been traced through these pages. If you don't ask that question consciously, the surrounding culture will answer it for you through its unconscious addiction to money, power, and individualistic glory. You will be subsumed, with a false self, entrenched in that lifeless way of living.

Asking that question at the beginning of your quest, when your life is awakening toward a call to your true self, will help you rest in a grace beyond yourself. And on your journey, as you ask that question again, repeatedly, you will find what you need to take the next step forward. But where will you find the answers? Certainly wisdom will come to you from many diverse sources. But one source that still resonates today came first in a letter to a group struggling to internalize a radically new understanding of God, the world, and Jesus in the city of Ephesus nineteen-hundred years ago:

> I bow my knees before the Father, from whom every family in heaven and on earth takes its name. I pray that, according to the riches of his glory, he may grant that you may be strengthened in your inner being with power through his Spirit, and that Christ may dwell in your hearts through faith, as you are being rooted and grounded in love. I pray that you may have the power to comprehend, with

> all the saints, what is the breadth and length and height and depth, and to know the love of Christ that surpasses knowledge, so that you may be filled with all the fullness of God. (Eph 3:14–19)

The call is for your inner being to be rooted and grounded in love. And that, of course, is a lifelong journey, beginning when you discover, in moments of graced awakenings, that this love has already embraced you. Responding to this call presents you with great risks. But the risk/reward ratio, in the end, is off the charts. You are rooting your life in the hope that this love is at the center of all things. In this place Frederick Buechner's words are worth remembering: "To say that God is love is either the last straw or the ultimate truth."

Your holding space provides the opening to internalize the immensity of this love—to comprehend how high it reaches, how deep it goes, how wide it stretches, and how long it endures. This love overwhelms your understanding, shatters your restrictive categories, breaks open your heart, and animates your vision. Maybe it's something like hearing your favorite piece of music in surround sound with the volume turned up all the way. You don't just listen. Your whole body, your soul, seem to reverberate it on every level.

The problem, of course, is that over the course of history institutionalized Christianity has turned the volume down, removed some speakers, muffled some of the words, and subdued the real message. You don't hear the full soundtrack.

But your holding space is the place where you can turn the volume back up, free from all the normal interference. When holding that space you'll sense yourself being asked, not whether you believe in Jesus, but whether in your soul you believe Jesus—that the words he shared, the life he lived, and the love he poured out to the end provide the story where you root and ground your life.

This makes a decisive difference in your outward action, because this love not only transforms your inner being. It also transforms the world.

The breadth, length, height, and depth of this love can never be constricted to just the human heart because it embraces the whole creation. What it touches it yearns to change and bring into the fullness intended by God. Rooted and grounded in this love, you will fearlessly confront all that perpetuates injustice, all that destroys creation, all that protects greed, and all that extols selfish ambition.

The love of God is immeasurable. Yet, it provides you with the measure for seeing all the dross that must be refined so the essence of all things can be revealed.

This love surpasses knowledge. You can't know it or contain it rationally. While it engages your mind, to take hold of it you must invite this love to grip your soul. You will get there, or it will get to you, more through practices of relinquishing than through thinking, more through abandonment than through achievement. It comes as your soul learns to dwell in belonging, connection, authenticity, and trust. And it requires what Søren Kierkegaard called a "leap of faith."

Think of your holding space as your own monastery or your place of retreat. This is the way you are set apart, where repeated practices subdue mental distraction, when silence becomes a welcomed gift, and when your true self finds the space and grace to emerge. There your soul can find its calling, its ministry, its way home.

Yet, this internal monastery or retreat space is never a place that cloisters you from the world's suffering and pain. James Finley shared in a meditation from the Center for Action and Contemplation what Thomas Merton once told him about the monastic life in the cloistered community of Gethsemani Abbey:

> We did not come here to breathe the rarified air beyond the suffering of this world. We came here to carry the suffering of the whole world into our heart. Otherwise there's no validity in living in a place like this.

The advantage of seeing your holding space as a distinct place of retreat, preparation, silence, and insight—your monastery—is that you know it always travels with you and that you can reenter it at any time. This treasured, protected space allows you to be rooted and grounded, again, in love. And that makes all the difference in the world, for the good of the world.

Epilogue

Your Anchorhold

In the convulsive time of the Middle Ages, some people took a radical step to become anchorites or anchoresses. Withdrawing from society, they permanently entered a cell, perhaps 8' x 15', often attached to the side of a church, and centered their life on prayer and the Eucharist. One window into the sanctuary opened to worship, food passed through another window, and a third opened to the outside. These cells were called anchorholds, and thousands of them were inhabited, often placed in the heart of a community. More women than men were attracted to this calling. Though living in monastic separation, their example and wisdom often became a spiritual center for others. Ordinary people, bishops, and even kings would come to seek counsel. Anchorites and anchoresses played an influential role in recentering a holy vision of the intentions of God's love for society from those small cells.

Now is a time of severe social turmoil, growing global threats, and debilitating political alienation where an onslaught of threats to the most vulnerable groups in society and a determined effort to mobilize public fear and bigotry in the service of political aggrandizement are rampant. Much of the American church has been captured in a cult of personality magnifying exclusionary nationalistic loyalties. Throughout the world authoritarianism is ascendant, accompanied by worsening economic inequalities and pending climate catastrophe. This setting is where you are endeavoring to find your voice, exercise your witness, listen for God's call, and discern your vocation.

It's important to ask yourself, "Where is my anchorhold?" This is another way of exploring whether you have a holding space that will serve and sustain you in your necessary soulwork of justice. That's the primary question for you to face. So much that follows in your life will depend on your answer.

Julian of Norwich lived as an anchoress at the end of the fourteenth century. You've probably heard of her and her widely known phrase, "All shall be well," from her book, *The Revelations of Divine Love*. But a context for her writing and this line matters. She was writing in a time when the bubonic plague was killing thousands. The Hundred Years' War was being waged between France and England. The Archbishop of Canterbury was murdered, and rival popes were excommunicating one another. Fears, suffering, and death were carried deep into Julian's anchorhold by those seeking her spiritual guidance. All of these things permeated her life of prayer. With the words she offered others, Julian wasn't sharing some pious escape from brutal realities. Rather, she was calling those who turned to her wisdom and revelations to discover a deep grounding in God's mysterious love that would hold them with faithful confidence in the center of the world's pain, and their own.

That is your calling in this hour, and in the days and years ahead. Be anchored, so you can give to others what they most need. And so you can view the world through the lens of God's love and act accordingly.

You are called to be a friend and follower of Jesus who discovers your life is embedded deeply in God's presence; this has a transforming impact on others and awakens all you encounter to the divine Love that suffers with and heals the world's pain.

The tools for your holding space and anchorhold are at your disposal, and four essential movements to guide your soul's journey have been outlined. As you stop denying your shadow, you will no longer project it onto others.

These prepare you to embrace your deepest identity as being in solidarity with the world. As a follower of Jesus, you participate in love that is poured out for the life of the world. In the chaotic, disintegrating tumult of our time, you can pray to be a vessel for leaven, salt, and light to enter the world, even if only as a mustard seed, knowing that this love holds the power to transform.

You will see the world, at its core, as beloved by God. You'll know what can be because this already is true. And like the prophet, you then can welcome the future, longing and living for the day that will surely be, when "the earth shall be full . . . of the glory of God as the waters cover the sea" (Hb 2:14). That's what it means to become usable for God.

This beloved, broken world needs you. And yes, God is inviting and beckoning you into a surrendered life. I pray you will do whatever you need to do, to come, taste and see this life.

In this book's opening I urged you, if you felt moved at all, simply to take a step forward. Since then, I've tried to describe the path ahead—what you might expect, and how you can prepare yourself. Now, at the close of this book, I'm making an appeal. Embark on this inward and outward journey. Learn how to sink your work for justice in the thirst of your soul to abide in God's love. Dwell there.

And as you dwell there, you can expect to dream dreams, and maybe even see visions. After Thomas Merton had his pivotal conversion at Fourth and Walnut Street in Louisville, he described what he experienced in his *Conjectures of a Guilty Bystander:*

> At the center of our being is a point of nothingness which is untouched by sin and by illusion, a point of pure truth, a point or spark which belongs entirely to God, which is never at our disposal, from which God disposes of our lives, which is inaccessible to the fantasies of our own mind or the brutalities of our own will. This little point of nothingness and of absolute poverty is the pure glory of God in us. . . . It is like a pure diamond, blazing with the invisible light of heaven. It is in everybody, and if we could see it we would see these billions of points of light coming together in the face and blaze of a sun that would make all the

> darkness and cruelty of life vanish completely. . . .
> I have no program for this seeing. It is only given.
> But the gate of heaven is everywhere.

That pure diamond, refined gold, is there, planted by God at your deepest self. And it does open a gateway to the essence of abundant life flowing through all creation. Gordon Cosby preached about this stream of living waters in November 1986 at Church of the Saviour. I pray these words resonate in your soul:

> Don't you know there is a limitless flow of life—a superabundance of love and caring? You simply cannot exhaust it. It may be tough learning how to touch that current, how to get into that stream, to feel the flow and power of it, to be carried by it, but one thing is sure: the stream is there. And it is limitless.

My friend, wade into this stream.

Sources

Chapter II: Your Leap of Change

"*Only the pain we name is available for transformation.*"
Kelley Nikondeha, *The First Advent in Palestine* (Minneapolis: Broadleaf Books, 2022), 21.

"*Clad in this 'self,' the creation of irresponsible and ignorant persons…*"
Dag Hammarskjold, *Markings* (New York: Alfred A. Knopf, 1967), 152.

"*What happens in psychotherapy? We ask the question…*"
Quoted by Chuck DeGroat, October 25, 2022, on Twitter (X).

Chapter III: Holding the Space

"*Wes Michaelson—one of the cadre of 'Whiz Kids' helping their Senators…*"
George Wilson, *Washington Post,* August 4, 1969.

"*As we become aware of the shadow side…*"
Thomas Keating, *Divine Therapy and Addiction: Centering Prayer and the Twelve Steps* (New York: Lantern Books, 2009), 157–58.

Chapter IV: From Self-Sufficiency to Belonging

"*…necessity never to need anybody…*"
Karen Horney, *Self-Analysis* (New York: W. H. Norton and Company, 1942; Norton paperback 1968, reissued 1994), 55.

"...many Indigenous communities consider..."
Elizabeth Dias, "When Does Life Begin?" *New York Times*, December 31, 2022.

"It's hard in our self-promoting culture to confess..."
Debie Thomas, *Into the Mess and Other Jesus Stories: Reflections on the Life of Christ* (Eugene, OR: Cascade Books, 2022), 146.

"So it is that we in the graced moments of our awaking..."
Jame Finley, *The Healing Path: A Memoir and an Invitation* (Maryknoll, NY: Orbis Books, 2023), 120.

"Little did I know that as I learned to gaze..."
Finley, *The Healing Path*, 62.

Chapter V: From Certainty to Connection

"One of the first lessons we all must learn..."
Estelle Frankel, *The Wisdom of Not Knowing: Discovering a Life of Wonder by Embracing Uncertainty* (Boulder, CO: Shambhala, 2017), 43.

"Knowledge is fostered by curiosity..."
Abraham J. Heschel, *Who Is Man?* (Stanford, CA: Stanford University Press, 1965), 89.

"A terrible lust for certitude..."
Richard Rohr, "Perfection Is Practicing Love," *Daily Meditations,* Center for Action and Contemplation, March 13, 2023.

"As every psychotherapist knows..."
John Sanford, *Mystical Christianity: A Psychological Commentary on the Gospel of John* (New York: The Crossroad Publishing Company, 1993), 34.

"The story of Christianity moves...."
Robert Webber, *Ancient-Future Faith: Rethinking Evangelism for a Postmodern Generation* (Grand Rapids, MI: Baker Academic, 1999), 16.

Chapter VI: From Grandiosity to Authenticity

"…a very ancient Christian tool for the discernment of spirits…"
Richard Rohr and Andreas Ebert, *The Enneagram: A Christian Perspective* (New York: The Crossroad Publishing Company, 2013), xvi–xvii.

"As children Threes were often loved…"
Rohr and Ebert *The Enneagram*, 81.

"The face of narcissism often looks like…"
Chuck DeGroat, *When Narcissism Comes to Church: Healing Your Community from Emotional and Spiritual Abuse* (Downers Grove, IL: IVP, 2020), 50.

"As the Beloved, I can confront…"
Henri J. M. Nouwen, *The Return of the Prodigal Son: A Story of Homecoming* (New York: Doubleday, 1994), 39.

"The sustained practice of contemplation…"
Richard Rohr, "Right Here, Right Now," *Daily Meditations*, Center for Action and Contemplation, July 11, 2024.

"Simon: And as you say, the lessons…"
NPR, *Weekend Edition*, July 6, 2024.

"Sacha Pfeiffer: You also note that survival…"
NPR, *Morning Edition*, July 10, 2024.

Chapter VII: From Control to Trust

"What you can plan is too small for you to live."
David Whyte, "What to Remember upon Waking," *The House of Belonging* (Langley, WA: Many Rivers Press, 2002), 26.

"The fundamental and paradoxical premise…"
Rami Shapiro, *Recovery, the Sacred Art: The Twelve Steps as Spiritual Practice* (Woodstock, VT: Skylight Paths, 2009), 3.

"All great spirituality is about letting go."
　　Richard Rohr, "The Spirituality of Letting Go," *Daily Meditations*, Center for Action and Contemplation, April 23, 2023.

"In the tradition of Celtic monasticism…"
　　Christine Valters Paintner, "Pilgrimage of Resurrection: Wandering for the Love of God," *Pathos*, April 24, 2015.

"God asks only that you get out of God's way…"
　　Meister Eckhart, Sermon on 1 John 4:9, from Richard Rohr, "The Spirituality of Letting Go," *Daily Meditations,* Center for Action and Contemplation, April 23, 2023.

"If life, as we experience it, is a fragile…"
　　Barbara Holmes, *Crisis Contemplation: Healing for a Wounded Village* (Albuquerque, NM: CAC Publications, 2021), 9–10, 45.

"We must travel inward, into the interior depth…"
　　Ilia Delio, *The Hours of the Universe: Reflections on God, Science, and the Human Journey* (Maryknoll, NY: Orbis Books, 2021), 105–6.

"There is no excuse which permits us to avoid…"
　　Paul Tillich, *The Shaking of the Foundations* (New York, Charles Scribner's and Sons, 1948; republished Eugene, OR: Wipf and Stock, 2011).

"I started showing up for every person…"
　　Adam Bucko, *Let Your Heartbreak Be Your Guide: Lessons in Engaged Contemplation* (Maryknoll, NY: Orbis Books, 2022), 116–17.

Chapter VIII: Gathered Wisdom

"The habit of discernment is a quality…"
　　Ruth Haley Barton, *Sacred Rhythms: Arranging Our Lives for Spiritual Transformation* (Downers Grove, IL: IVP, 2006), 111.

"Attention is a limited resource, so pay attention…"
　　Howard Rheingold, AZQuotes.com, Wind and Fly LTD (2025).

Sources

"Distractedness was a kind of preexisting condition…"
Jamie Kreiner, *The Wandering Mind: What Medieval Monks Tell Us About Distraction* (New York: Liveright Publishing Corporation, 2023), 10.

"It [distraction] had also come to signal…"
Kreiner, *The Wandering Mind*, 12.

"The function of contemplation…"
Parker Palmer, *The Active Life: A Spirituality of Work, Creativity, and Caring* (San Francisco: Harper and Row, 1990), 25.

"Traditionally…prophets were mystics…"
Albert Nolan, *Jesus Today: A Spirituality of Radical Freedom* (Maryknoll, NY: Orbis Books, 2006), 72.

"Everything begins in mysticism and ends in politics."
Charles Péguy, *Notre Jeunesse* (Cahiers de la Quinzaine: 1910), 27. Original text: *"Tout commence en mystique et finit en politique."*

"We don't often look at white supremacy…"
Interview of Rahiel Tesfamariam by Darren Saint-Ulysse, "We Know This Is Not Our Home," *Sojourners* 53, no. 9 (November 2024): 30, 31.

"It's often said that pursuing disarmament is naive…"
Archbishop John Wester, "What Conversations Can We Start on Nuclear Disarmament?, address to Catholic Worker national gathering, October 4, 2024.

"Eights are self-confident, strong, and assertive."
Enneagram Type Eight: The Challenger, The Enneagram Institute.

"The more Eights build up their egos…"
Enneagram Type Eight.

"Unless we are led to some kind of contemplative…"
Richard Rohr, "Peacemaking and Contemplation," *Daily Meditations*, Center for Action and Contemplation, September 24, 2024.

"To say that God is love…"
 Frederick Buechner. Quoted September 10, 2017.

"We did not come here to breathe the rarified air…"
 James Finley, "Not for Ourselves Alone," *Daily Meditations*, Center for Action and Contemplation, July 26, 2024.

Epilogue

"At the center of our being…"
 Thomas Merton, *Conjectures of a Guilty Bystander* (New York: Doubleday and Company, 1965, 1966), 142.

"Don't you know there is…"
 Gordon Cosby, "Abundant Streams of Living Water," *Inward/Outward Together,* Church of the Saviour, March 16, 2023.

Acknowledgments

The genesis of this book came during COVID when my wife, Kaarin, suggested that I read through all the journals I had kept for over fifty years. She wondered if there were things worth passing on to our two children. Doing so took a year and led to the discovery of insights and movements in my inward journey that seemed to hold wider truths worth sharing. In the resulting development of this book, Kaarin has been a steadfast advocate, counselor, and encourager, for which I am forever grateful.

I've often said, there is no good writing. There is only good rewriting. This book proved that point numerous times. Kathy Helmers, an exceptional literary agent, helped organize, focus, and distill its core message, testing this with others and serving like a manuscript's midwife. Several trusted friends were invaluable in reading evolving drafts and providing their responses, including Bill and Karen Thompson, San and Jan Williams, Jon Pott, Fr. Joel Gardner, Brian McLaren, Stacey Duensing Pearce, and Jeri Eckhart-Queenan.

Orbis Books has become such a hospitable and supportive home for this book. It fits with their rich and splendid family of titles that bring a focus on spirituality and justice, and I'm deeply grateful for their support. Lil Copan, my editor, has brought her amazing skills to this manuscript with her ability to hone and curate thousands of words with discerning clarity. She has the gift of asking broad questions about what should be included and then using exacting precision on how each line should read.

My desire to integrate an outward journey of activism and witness with an inward journey of spiritual grounding and authenticity began at Church of the Saviour in Washington, DC, early in my adult life. I am indebted to that community for demonstrating how Christian faith can become incarnated and real, nurturing my own lifelong pathway that is reflected in these pages. Gordon Cosby and Elizabeth O'Connor were early mentors, and friends today including Rebecca Vargas and Basil Buchanan continue that legacy and consistently encouraged my writing.

Richard Rohr and the Center for Action and Contemplation in Albuquerque have provided an ongoing reservoir of spiritual wisdom and nourishment. Rohr's Daily Meditations have frequently suggested openings that I have pursued in refining this book.

The Norbertine Santa Maria de la Vid Abbey outside Albuquerque has been a destination for retreat and a place to sequester myself for writing at some critical points. I've always been welcomed there by former Abbot Joel Garnder and the community.

In Santa Fe, Mille is a French bakery and café. A back booth by the wall served as a frequent site for writing and editing, always undisturbed, except for a vanilla latte and a croissant. Those croissants are the best in Santa Fe, made from organic stone-ground flour and butter imported from France. Marcel Remillieux, the gifted chef and owner, and the staff extend classic hospitality and helped this book more than they will know. If you come to Santa Fe, pay a visit.